ECLIPSE OF THE SUNNIS

ECLIPSE
OF THE
SUNNIS

*Power, Exile, and
Upheaval in the
Middle East*

DEBORAH AMOS

PublicAffairs
New York

PublicAffairs books are available at special discounts for bulk purchases
in the U.S. by corporations, institutions, and other organizations. For
more information, please contact the Special Markets Department at the
Perseus Books Group, 2300 Chestnut Street, Suite 200, Philadelphia,
PA 19103; call (800) 810-4145, ext. 5000; or e-mail
special.markets@perseusbooks.com.

Book Design by Timm Bryson

Library of Congress Cataloging-in-Publication Data
    Amos, Deborah.
    Eclipse of the Sunnis : power, exile, and upheaval in the Middle East /
Deborah Amos.—1st ed.
    p. cm.
    ISBN 978-1-58648-649-5 (hardcover)
    1. Sunnites—Middle East—Social conditions. 2. Sunnites—Social
conditions—Iraq. 3. Iraq War, 2003—Refugees—Middle East. 4. Iraq
War, 2003—Social aspects. 5. Sunnites—Relations—Shi'ah. 6. Shi'ah—
Relations—Sunnites. I. Title.
DS59.S86A66 2010
956.7044'3086914—dc22
                                                    2009039950
First Edition
10 9 8 7 6 5 4 3 2 1

TO R.C. DAVIS

who makes it all possible in this lifetime adventure

Tu lascerai ogne cosa diletta
più caramente; e questo è quello strale
che l'arco de lo essilio pria saetta.
Tu proverai sì come sa di sale
lo pane altrui, e come è duro calle
lo scendere e 'l salir per l'altrui scale. . . .

You shall leave everything you love most;
this is the arrow that the bow of exile
shoots first. You are to know the bitter taste
of others' bread, how salty it is, and know
how hard a path it is for one who goes
ascending and descending others' stairs. . . .

—DANTE

A man must put his faith in his country, his
family, and his money. The better alternative,
when a man cannot defend any of these
things, is to go to a safe place.

—AHMED AL-QUSY,
IRAQI EXILE IN DAMASCUS

CONTENTS

INTRODUCTION

It was easy to believe, as we watched U.S. President Barack Hussein Obama stride across the stage at Cairo University on June 4, 2009, that a new era was about to begin between the United States and the Middle East. The campus was a symbolic backdrop. Founded in 1908 as a secular center of learning, the university serves as an intellectual bridge between East and West. The campus had boiled with anti-American sentiment during the U.S.-led invasion of Iraq, but on this day the keen anticipation was palpable as the audience waited for an American president to give what was expected to be a historic address to the Muslim world.

The president's name alone had resonance: Some Cairo newspapers even went so far as to suggest that he was America's first Muslim president, in keeping with the Arab tradition that a father's religion is conferred upon the son. Of course, in American tradition, identity is a much more fluid concept. We wear our identities lightly, easily adding or shedding to suit the circumstances. So it was that an American president with a Muslim pedigree addressed the most deeply disruptive question of identity in the region where identity colors politics most. In his message to the faithful, President Obama exhorted that "the fault lines must be closed among Muslims" and he especially noted the fault lines between Shiite and Sunni, a historic chasm, often dormant, newly pried open by the U.S.-led war in Iraq. The divide that has seeped into the social fabric of the region is not principally about religion, but about power and the vacuum created when an American army toppled a Sunni tyrant. The immediate opportunity this offered to Iraq's Shiite community was well understood. Ever since the failure of the George H. W. Bush administration to support the Shiite rising against Saddam in 1991, Americans had recognized the potential for an alliance with the Shiite majority against Saddam. Excluded from U.S. thinking ahead of the war in 2003 was the ripple of consequences across all Sunni communities in the Middle East that Saddam's removal would create. That is the subject of this book.

Closing the fault lines between Shiite and Sunni must begin in Iraq, but Mr. Obama hardly mentioned the place where the Sunni-Shiite divide is the most acute. Elsewhere, the signs in the region were much more uplifting: The Lebanese dented Hezbollah's popularity by voting for a publicly pro-American political coalition in a parliamentary election. Millions of Iranians bravely took to the streets to challenge the rigged election of a radical president. Syria celebrated the announcement of the return of an American ambassador after a four-year hiatus, a concrete sign that America was offering an open hand to adversaries. But the Iraqis were not yet part of the recovery. Despite an overall reduction in violence in Iraq, one statistic remains troubling and has barely changed. As of 2009, of the two million Iraqis who fled the country, only about 5 percent have returned. The fundamental problems that fueled the insurgency and the civil war are unresolved, as the exiles know all too well.

An estimated 60 percent of the refugees are Sunni Arabs. Fifteen percent are Iraqi Christians. Secular Shiites, Mandaeans, Yazidis, and Kurds are adrift, too, the losers in a brutal civil war that sealed the power of Shiite nationalists. Yet the sectarian nature of the crisis has been largely overlooked. This shifting population is a huge loss to Iraq, a vast problem to neighboring governments, a collective tragedy for many caught up in it, and a significant indicator of the health, stability, and viability of Iraq and the Middle East. The newly stateless have become the most important indicator of the next phase of the region's history. In their individual stories are found the religious, tribal, and sectarian challenges and conflicts that must somehow be settled for the violence to end.

While five million Iraqis had left or been driven out of Iraq during Saddam's three decades in power, theirs was a slow-motion outflow of political dissidents. With the U.S. occupation, the collapse of the Iraqi state, and the violent power struggle that followed, almost as many millions were displaced in under five years, across borders and inside the country. The migration began as a trickle in 2004, when the driving force was criminal kidnapping gangs and Sunni insurgent attacks. The movement accelerated in 2006 with Al Qaeda's bombing of the Golden Dome mosque in Samarra, Iraq—an attack on a revered Shiite religious site that unleashed a wave of Shiite revenge attacks against Sunnis across the country. Displacements rose again through 2007 in a final spasm of sectarian cleansing even as 30,000 additional U.S. troops were deployed in Iraq.

The only way to explain the calamity was in the daily details, the particular threats that propelled the politics of displacement and made the bigger picture understandable. I began a journey to document the mass departure, traveling to Damascus, Amman, and Beirut to interview the growing exile population.

There are no camps of any kind in this latest wave of the dispossessed. The largest numbers quietly settled in the poor suburbs surrounding Arab capitals. I had seen them at the Baghdad airport in tearful good-bye embraces, well-dressed families struggling with luggage that was now the sum of their lives. Others drove west out of the capital along the desert road, the five hundred heartbreaking miles to Jordan's border. When Jordan sealed the border against the human tide, the exodus turned north for the fourteen-hour drive to Syria. The Iraqi exiles brought money or gold, or relied on extended families to support what many believed would be a short stay until the storms of violence passed at home. They waited long past the time when the money ran out.

It was an exodus of the professional class—doctors, scientists, poets, professors, actors, even artisans, all of whom were the best hope to remake Iraq into the democratic and prosperous symbol of America's most ambitious early dream. An unprecedented brain drain in the oil industry created an expertise deficit when more than half of the top one hundred managers fled. Iraqi government ministers began to complain of a shortage of workers able to write contracts. Scientists left the country, preferring unemployment in exile over joblessness and fear at home. The exodus continued down through the ranks of the middle class, including the workers in the vast government bureaucracy. By 2007, the overwhelming majority of exiles, more than 70 percent, were professionals and technocrats from Baghdad. Their departure crippled the government back home.

"To be honest with you, I didn't want to be a body in a plastic bag. I preferred to stay alive," explained Mohammed Yahya, an English-speaking college-educated veterinarian who had been grateful for a job with a U.S. contractor in 2003. He had worked inside Baghdad's "Green Zone" in Iraq's Finance Ministry for eighteen months. But when some of his Iraqi colleagues were threatened, then killed, he decided that translating for a British news organization was a far safer occupation. By the summer of 2007, after another series of threats, Mohammed Yahya was certain he had to leave the country to survive.

Nezar Hussein, a twenty-seven-year-old filmmaker, stayed in Baghdad longer than most of his friends but as the U.S. surge of troops in Baghdad reached full strength he crossed the Syrian border, finally driven out by the furious battles in his neighborhood, the Karada district in central Baghdad. Before his departure, he posted on the Internet his fearful account of how, for his own survival, he was finally forced to carry a weapon:

> It's three o'clock in the morning and the sound of mortars and Katyusha rockets are my soundtrack. All I know for a fact is that gunmen are touring the city, killing without mercy. I am writing now with a loaded Russian-made rifle next to me. There are lots of bullets waiting in my camera case; I hope they stay waiting. It is chaos out there; many killings—too many. The dead are numerous, and the living are just waiting their turn. It is a cinematic scene, and everyone is waiting for a role.

Forced into exile, Nezar Hussein was not comfortable in the role of refugee. He refused to sign up at the United Nations office in Damascus. His plan was to return, eventually.

Approximately one in six Iraqis had become a refugee or was displaced. The equivalent number in terms of the American population would be fifty million men, women, and children.

Their absence was remaking Iraq and was shifting the politics of the countries to which they had relocated. To understand why they left and why they had been targeted, I believed, would lead to an understanding of what it would take to get them to go back. In relative safety—in cafés, on thin mats in bare rented rooms, and in nightclubs—I listened to accounts of what had happened to them. I collected hundreds of stories. Nearly everyone had an account of kidnapping, torture, extortion, rape, and death threats that had forced them to run for their lives. An Iraqi blogger captured the pain of departure when he wrote, "So here is why I left Iraq: For no crime at all but being a Sunni. . . . One of my friends keeps berating me about how I should love this country, the land of my ancestors where I was born and raised; how I should be grateful and return to the place that gave me everything. I always tell him the same thing. Iraq as you and I once knew it is lost. What is left of it, I don't want."

One question this book asks is whether there is any prospect that "restoration" is possible or even desired by the government in Baghdad. As the exiles look for a sign of government concern for their plight, they were not reassured by the record at the Ministry of Displacement. In the summer of 2009, the Ministry, underfunded and understaffed, exhausted the budget for resettling the internally displaced. The government program, as well as large scale exile returns, was on hold.

The refugees raise fundamental questions about Iraq's identity. The return of the exiles, then, is more than a symbolic act of reconciliation: It would represent a fundamental decision about Iraq's regional identity. If the exiles return and flourish, then a broadly secular, modern nation could reassert itself in place of warring sectarian factionalism. For this to happen, the Sunni eclipse would have to be reconciled.

In the meantime, Iraq's poorest neighbors are bearing the legacy of a war they opposed. While Syrian officials cannot calculate the exact number of Iraqi refugees crowding schools and hospitals and straining the social structure of the country, government departments have estimated an additional cost of a billion dollars a year to support Iraq's exile population. By crossing the Syrian border, Iraqis had left the hell of their old lives, but they soon discovered a different kind of hell. At the border, officials stamped Syrian policy into Iraqi passports in Arabic and English: "Employment Prohibited." Even if legal work were permitted, there were few job opportunities; unemployment in Syria was over 25 percent.

Jordanians resented the influx and blamed the new arrivals for rising prices, overcrowded schools, and an inflated housing market. Affordable apartments, a marriage prerequisite for young Arabs, disappeared from the market for Jordan's middle class. In the summertime, tap water dries up in a country with barely enough of this vital resource for the Jordanian population.

Jordan had been the traditional haven for Iraqis during Saddam's long rule. During the 1991 Gulf war, more than one million refugees crossed Jordan's border. That exodus included Egyptian workers,

Palestinians, and the survivors of an uprising when Iraqis responded to the American president's call to rise up against Saddam and the Republican Guards—a force the U.S. military left intact when it withdrew from Iraq. The Republican Guards slaughtered the rebels and drove out the surviving dissidents.

Jordanians loved Saddam. So Iraqi refugees made sure they remained practically unnoticed. Saddam came out on top of opinion polls even after he was dead, consistently beating out Osama bin Laden for the top spot. Jordan was a predominantly Sunni country and Saddam had been good to Jordan, buying favorable coverage by showering local journalists with cash and cars. In the 1990s, Saddam pumped free oil into Jordan's economy, which softened the burden of the exile population of the time. But Saddam was gone and Jordan had empty pockets for the new wave of mostly Sunni refugees fleeing from a neighboring state that for the first time in history was dominated by Iraq's Arab Shiites.

This new exodus was not the narrative that the Bush administration wanted to project, or acknowledge, and remained invisible for much of the world. The U.S. security plan known as the surge was an American success story, but it was a sideshow for those forced out of homes and neighborhoods in a power struggle that used displacement and exile as a weapon. More Iraqis left the country in 2007 than in 2006, the year that the surge got under way. The International Organization for Migration, a UN-affiliated agency on the ground in Iraq, was tracking widespread displacements in 2007; the movement inside the country had increased by a factor of 20. Thirty thousand additional U.S. troops, spread out across Baghdad, brought no return of the exiles. Political reconciliation at the highest levels of the Iraqi government was at a standstill; on the ground the Sunni-Shiite divide was still steeped in blood.

The only Iraqis who regularly went back home were the fighters—those who had joined the Sunni insurgency or the Shiite militias. They freely crossed borders for rest and recuperation. I encountered some of them in Damascus—hard, suspicious men who defined themselves as nationalists or Islamists or both. Practical men, they also wanted to resettle wives and children to a safe place with a dependable school year. I met two Iraqi men in Damascus, a farmer who owned a large tract of land on the outskirts of Baghdad and a former government engineer with the Ministry of Industry. They were longtime friends and had joined a Sunni resistance group as the American tanks sped toward Baghdad in 2003. They were in Syria for a few weeks of vacation.

"We came here to get away from the pressure," the engineer told me, and he would soon go home to rejoin the fight.

Damascus was a haven for Shiite militants, too. Muqtada al-Sadr, the radical Shiite cleric who headed the largest militia in Iraq, had opened a branch office in Damascus so the city was often full of visiting Shiite militia men who had the cash for a few weeks of vacation in the summer. Damascus had much to offer for battle-weary young militants with free time. They arrived on the same big silver buses that dropped exhausted Iraqi passengers with overstuffed cloth suitcases into the Damascus suburbs. The permanent exiles feared these young men who had roundtrip plans, light luggage, and a self-certainty that set them apart.

There are so many Iraqis in outlying neighborhoods of the Syrian capital that some sections of the city were indistinguishable from neighborhoods in Baghdad. The southern edge of Damascus became known as "Little Baghdad." Here groups of men gathered in one-room makeshift restaurants eating from plates piled high with lamb and rice. The names of the establishments paid tribute to a life left behind. One sign read "Fallujah" for the Sunni city of Western Iraq, but also for a city known to produce the best lamb kabob in the old Iraq. The cooks prepared food in the Iraqi tradition, adding extra lumps of white glistening fat to hunks of meat before shoveling the concoctions into a clay oven. The patrons talked in low voices, but the harsh Arabic accent spoken here was unmistakably Iraqi.

Farther south of Damascus another Iraqi neighborhood had sprung up around the shrine of Saida Zeinab, the granddaughter of the Prophet Muhammad. Fourteen hundred years ago, Zeinab's brother Imam Hussein was killed in Karbala, in what is now southern Iraq, by a murderous army sent by the powerful caliph in Damascus. The battle and Hussein's martyrdom mark the historic Sunni-Shiite rift and form the narrative of betrayal, guilt, and loss that is the bedrock of Shiite religious traditions. The shrine of Saida Zeinab has been a destination for Shiite religious pilgrimages for centuries.

Inside the shrine, a vast carpeted room punctuated by marble columns, is the place where Saida Zeinab is buried. A large ornate silver box is believed to hold her remains. When I visited, Shiite pilgrims quietly prayed alone and in groups, or sat for hours in the cool carpeted room. Women took turns approaching the silver box, weeping. In sing-song rhythms, they chanted the mourning prayers for Zeinab's suffering and their own.

For years, the religious tourist traffic had come primarily from Iran's Shiites, but now Iraqi Shiites dominated the religious processions and commemorations in the neighborhood surrounding the shrine. On the streets outside, buses had the distinctive red license plates from Iraq. In the shops lining the entrance to the shrine, Iraqi flags were on sale and young Iraqi boys begged for spare change.

Many of the older exiles lacked survival skills. They had been teachers and government bureaucrats in Baghdad. Educated people, they did not know how to plaster a wall or have the stamina for a twelve-hour day in a factory. Children had a better chance of work in the grey economy, skipping school to sell phone cards or to tend the *narguila*, the tobacco-filled water pipes in street restaurants.

Generally, however, families with children had a particularly difficult time: They needed bigger and more expensive apartment space. Then there was the question of schooling. Entrance into Syria's education system required enormous patience. Permissions were needed from at least three ministries, which could take days of waiting in line to get the proper authorization. Enrolling a child in the Syrian system incurred additional costs in school uniforms and books. But enrollment could be derailed if the family had neglected to include school records when packing up for a panicked flight out of the country. Most Iraqis carried their past lives in plastic bags—house deeds, school records, employment recommendations, birth certificates, photographs.

Life was hard for almost every exile in Damascus, but single women with children had the toughest time. Um Nour, a single mother, left after her husband abandoned her and the Shiite militia that controlled her neighborhood doused her with acid. A Sunni, with a Shiite husband, she was a target for sectarian cleansing. Mixed marriages—between Shiites and Sunnis—were not uncommon in the urban-educated population in Baghdad during Saddam's time. In fact, the label *mixed marriage* came to be used only after 2003, when Iraqis adopted more sectarian identities—a process that often tore families apart. The new rules of the sectarian divide were hardest for women. The norms of traditional culture unraveled as wives and widows of mixed marriages were rejected by their own families and their in-laws for marrying outside their sect. Abandoned, severed from social systems, these women were left to fend for themselves with young children to care for.

When Um Nour first arrived in Damascus with her two children, she quickly found a job at a beauty salon working with Iraqi hairdressers who had set up shop for the exile population. The beauty salon was a front for prostitution. Sex work was a desperate solution for women who had nothing else to sell. The social judgments of Baghdad were easily abandoned in the anonymity and poverty of Damascus. When she first arrived, solicitations for sex were often crudely conducted on the streets. The business quickly moved to late-night clubs.

Um Nour's own daughter was still in school, a luxury based on her mother's earning. "My daughter, I do not let her mix with the clients. I tell her this business is bad. She doesn't know that I work at the nightclubs."

On the way out of the apartment I noticed a small picture of Saddam Hussein under the television set. He was smiling. It was the only photograph Um Nour had brought with her from Iraq.

Many Iraqi exiles were too traumatized to go home. A safe but airless apartment in Damascus was the preferred place to erase the memory of a terrorizing ordeal that had revealed the darkest side of human nature. Others, who arrived less damaged, but still desperate, had made decisions in Damascus that would forever taint their lives and make it impossible to go back.

As for the rest, there were too many reasons not to return. Sunnis, in contact with relatives back home, deeply insecure and largely excluded from power at every level, waited for the Shiite-dominated government to show signs of political reconciliation. Iraqis who had worked for the Americans waited for the death lists to disappear. Secular exiles waited for assurances that the country would not become an Islamic state. Couples in mixed marriages waited, too, until it was safe to be a Sunni married to a Shiite. Christians, Mandeans, and Yazidis—Iraqi's non-Muslim minorities—believed Iraq's extreme religious leaders wanted to cleanse the country of non-Muslims. They all believed that Iraq had been transformed into a country they no longer recognized. They waited to see if their Iraq would indeed be restored, or if it had been erased.

Little of this found its way into President Obama's speech at Cairo University. It is a narrative missing in the American discussion about Iraq. Instead we told ourselves a different story: Iraq was a mess on the verge of collapse and America was losing the war when a brilliant general stepped in at the last minute and deployed American troops and matériel to sort out the problem in the can-do American way. The story had a nicely macho name: the surge. In our enthusiasm for this version of events and by mistakenly making the story about us and not Iraq we have overlooked the fact that there was a surge in the other direction—out of Iraq. For Iraqis the "surge" story was one of departure, not only of the arrival of additional U.S. troops. This is the story we have not dealt with.

In 2009, for the first time since the war began, an American administration acknowledged the refugee crisis. When President Barack Obama announced a timetable for U.S. withdrawal from Iraq he described the refugees as "a challenge to the stability of the region." He evoked images of the restive Palestinians and Afghans who had produced a vengeful and angry generation in other refugee camps that have roiled the region to this day. Iraq's refugees are a problem, but they are also a resource, an educated middle class yearning for an Iraq that values their skills and offers a future for their children. Without a solution, Iraq will remain unstable and the Obama administration won't be able responsibly to extract U.S. troops from the region.

The journey undertaken for this book has been to a virtual Iraq, one that exists beyond its borders, in refugee communities across the region. Iraqis are tied to their homeland through technology that Saddam denied them and the U.S. invasion made possible. There is no model for this middle-class exodus in the Arab world. In chat rooms and on cellphones, web cameras, and blogs, a larger Iraq exists. The community of exiles is in daily contact waiting for word from home that it is time to come back. The rest of the region is waiting, too.

CHAPTER ONE

SELLING THE COUNTRY

Damascus is a city filled with a longing for its past greatness. Poets have called Damascus the "Paradise of the Orient," the "Bride of All Cities." In the seventh and eighth centuries, the city was the capital of the Umayyad empire, the Islamic caliphate that eventually stretched from Spain to India. According to Christian myth, Damascus was the original Garden of Eden; according to Islamic history, the place where Cain murdered Abel. Damascus has claims on being the oldest continuously inhabited city on Earth, a status Mark Twain acknowledged in his book *Innocents Abroad*, written after he visited the city in the 1860s: "No recorded event has occurred in the world but Damascus was in existence to receive news of it. Go back as far as you will into the vague past, there was always a Damascus. She has looked upon the dry bones of a thousand empires and will see the tombs of a thousand before she dies." A war and an exodus of refugees were another chapter in the city's long history.

Modern Damascus, which sprawls across a plain at the foot of Mount Qassioun, is now a shabbier paradise despite its wide French-designed boulevards and tree-lined avenues. Culturally, Damascus is a secular and tolerant city. Friday prayers are packed, but so are Damascus nightclubs. On weekends, Damascenes crowd the streets in the latest Western fashions, with an even mix of men and women. I would pack my long black *abaya* and head scarf out of habit from years of traveling in the region, but never needed them in Syria.

Syria is the only remaining Baathist regime in the world. There was some irony in the fact that so many Iraqis, who had lived for decades under the oppressive regime of Saddam and his Baath party, subsequently sought shelter in Syria, where the borders were open and no one was forced into a refugee camp. However, Arab countries, including Syria, did not officially recognize Iraqis as refugees. Damascus was not a signatory to the 1951 Convention Relating to the Status of Refugees. In Arab capitals, the exiles were referred to as "guests" or "visitors," with the same rights as any tourist. Iraqis were free to find accommodations they could afford, which often meant a place in one of the poor suburbs surrounding the capital. The family networks, so important in Middle East culture, were reconstituted in exile—as were the structures of a society that had been forced out of Baghdad.

Early in the spring of 2007, I joined a group of Iraqi actors in a rented ballroom in Damascus. The large room was luxurious, chosen as an example of excessive wealth. The gaudy interior was an imitation of Saddam Hussein's decorating style—too much was never enough, an approach also adopted by the new leaders of Iraq. The crystal chandeliers, ornate oversized mirrors, red-velvet wallpaper, and silk-covered chairs were a stark contrast to the abject living conditions of many of the actors in this room. They were refugees. Exiles. Homeless. But on this night, at least, they were re-creating a lost world.

I had come to watch the making of *Selling the Country*, a thirty-part comedy series, a broad and darkly satirical critique of the new Iraqi government, which was scheduled for broadcast during Ramadan later in the year. The holy month is a time when Muslims fast during the daylight hours and gather at dusk with family and friends to feast. In modern times, Ramadan is also a period in which to watch postprandial hours of television, prime-time viewing across the Muslim world. This was especially so for the intended audience in Iraq, where constant curfews and nighttime violence had kept the population at home after dark in the fall of 2007. Popular Ramadan television fare tended to be broad family dramas, little more than easily digestible soap operas. In the Arab world, theater was more often the protest medium, tolerated by autocrats because the message reached only an intimate, elite audience. But private satellite-television stations, unfiltered by state censorship, were changing the rules of the game. Subversive political theater could reach past an elite audience to the masses and, therefore, a work of art could be dangerous.

· The rehearsals in Damascus began at midnight so as not to disturb the late-dinner crowd of Syrian patrons at the restaurant next door. The rate to rent a ballroom was also cheaper late at night, and the hour was in keeping with the routines of the participants. The actors, producers, writers, makeup artists, dancers, and television technicians were all Iraqi refugees whose late-night lifestyle might be explained by the fact that when there is nothing to get up for, there is no hurry to get to bed.

The actors were some of Iraq's most famous faces, driven out of Baghdad because their profession had been considered anti-Islamic by extremists. Their flight was another sign of Iraq's tragedy, a cultural legacy lost. Crass, loud, and quick to laugh, they were the artistic elites of the exile community.

At the time of the American invasion, more than two dozen stages operated in Baghdad alone. Iraqi theater had developed into a cultural institution during Saddam's rule. Iraqi theater had built its reputation on comedies, but with the end of Saddam, plays had taken on a much darker edge. In "liberated" Iraq there were new freedoms to write, to act, to perform, to sing—but there was danger in these freedoms. Among other risks, they could trigger a death sentence from religious militants.

All of the actors in *Selling the Country* had long careers in Iraqi theater and television. Rasim al-Jumaily, sixty-nine, was the oldest in the troupe. A bald and portly man, he wore a crisp white military uniform the size of a tent, with a chest full of red battle ribbons. He was a natural comedian, with a wide jowly grin, stubby mustache, and wispy patches of white hair. Zuhair Rasheed, a character actor, was also instantly familiar to Iraqi audiences. He had played a six-foot-tall drag queen in a comedy show that was broadcast on Iraqi television soon after the U.S. occupation.

Mace Gomar, Iraq's professional "sexpot," a bottle blond with heavy eye makeup, was the only woman in a leading role. Well known for her work in television commercials, she wore a short, tight white uniform with black knee-high leather boots. She was the picture of a dominatrix; her exaggerated buxom figure was an ideal for a culture that had a love affair with eating.

I had met Mace a year earlier backstage at another production in Damascus appropriately titled *Homesick*. She appeared in the opening scene that featured a very small actor who had lost his pants and paraded on stage in red underwear and sneakers. The Iraqi audience returned night after night to pack the house. I could hear the sniffles around me as the audience—homesick themselves—wept in the dark. They had come to laugh, but always cried during the final scenes, because the play ends when everyone finally returns to Baghdad.

The mood in the exile community had grown more anxious and angry since then. Iraqis described themselves as being caught between three fires. They could no longer afford to stay in Damascus, it was still too dangerous to go home, and no other country wanted them. *Selling the Country* reflected the darker mood.

Iraqi law prohibited the broadcast of sarcastic images of government officials, a policy borrowed from Saddam's rules. But the media landscape and technology had changed since Saddam's time. Within the first year of the U.S. occupation almost every Iraqi house sprouted a satellite dish on the roof and the new Iraqi government could not control what citizens watched, especially the satellite programs originating from outside the country.

Selling the Country was sponsored by the satellite channel Al Sharqiya, headquartered in Dubai, which challenged Iraq's government-controlled television for viewers inside and outside the country. The station's owner, Saad Bazzaz, had learned the television business under Saddam Hussein. Bazzaz headed Iraq's state-controlled radio and television, but he broke with Saddam in 1992 and left the country. He was back soon after the Americans arrived to open Al Sharqiya TV, Iraq's first privately owned satellite channel. But Al Sharqiya earned a reputation among Shiite government officials as a "Sunni" channel because of its political content and Saudi investors. On the day Saddam was executed, Al Sharqiya's news presenters wore funereal black. The government banned the channel and closed its offices. But it is hard to exile satellite television stations. Bazzaz simply moved his operation to Dubai and continued to compete for the loyalty of Iraqi audiences. Often Al Sharqiya won the contest with witty comedies, contests, and reality shows. More important, Al Sharqiya offered a vision of Iraqi nationalism, an Iraqi identity that was more inclusive than the ultra-sectarian identity promoted by the politicians in Baghdad.

More than one hundred people had gathered in the Damascus ballroom, the actors happy to be together and working again. For some, it was their first paying job since fleeing their homeland. Some had brought family along and the ballroom had the feel of a class reunion. Ahmed Shukary al-Akeedy, a robust man with a taste for leather jackets and gold chains, was the executive producer. He was in his mid-forties, handsome in a soft way, with a chubby face and dark circles under his eyes. Akeedy had been involved in the theater since his early teens, interrupted only by mandatory military service. His father and his uncle had been pioneers of television drama in the 1950s, the pre-Saddam golden era, and had mentored many of Iraq's leading actors in programs at Baghdad's Fine Arts Academy.

As we waited for the production to begin, Akeedy told me that he had been on stage on March 20, 2003, the first night of the U.S. invasion. For Akeedy, the end of life as he knew it came when a security guard walked up on stage in Baghdad and announced, "The war has started." The guard then dismissed the audience and escorted the actors off the stage and into the unknown.

"We were saying good-bye. We didn't see the theater again. It was inside the Green Zone. I left my jacket there; it was like refusing to say the war had started. We were all crying." His eyes welled up as he remembered the abrupt departure. Akeedy's face, round and melancholy, lightened again when he explained the plot of the new production that savaged the shortcomings of the U.S.-backed government in Baghdad.

The series would take to task the Maliki government. The plot focused on government ministers who knew nothing about politics and everything about corruption. Episodes filled with clever ridicule were the first time Iraqi refugees had launched a broad critique of the government, and they gave voice to the frustrations of the exiles as well as many inside Iraq. The program had additional longevity in replays on YouTube. "Because of this government, I lost my brother," Akeedy said. Akeedy described his brother as a former member of Saddam's Baath party, a gentle man in Akeedy's memory, who had become a pharmacist after he left the army in the 1990s. But in the eyes of the Shiite sectarian militias in Iraq, there was no such thing as an ex-Baathist. Many were systematically hunted down and killed in revenge attacks that began in the months following the U.S. invasion. Some of the death squads came from Tehran. Other homegrown militias targeted former government officials, Baathist officials, and Sunni Muslims. Akeedy's brother had been on somebody's list.

Even after the death of his brother, Akeedy had not been ready to quit the new Iraq. The National Theater in Baghdad had reopened within weeks of the arrival of U.S. troops, although performances were restricted to occasional matinees because of the nighttime curfews. In 2004, Akeedy went to a meeting of actors at a Baghdad theater. "A man from the government arrived in a turban," Akeedy said with obvious disgust that a religious official was taking charge at the Ministry of Culture. "He said to us, 'I know you are from this sneaky, dirty place, but I welcome you.'" Even Saddam had showed more tolerance to the theater. Akeedy placed his hope in the elections promised for 2005. But at the same time he believed that the definitions of a new Iraq were being drawn. Iraq was transforming into a militantly sectarian religious country that would have no room for the secular artistic community that had defined his life. He finally fled to Damascus a year later, packing up his wife and three children.

By the spring of 2007, Akeedy and this troop of actors were ready to turn Iraq's tragedy into farce in the ballroom in Damascus. The scalding criticism was direct. The exodus out of Iraq was a scene played to great, and dark, comic effect: The sixty-nine-year-old actor Rasim al-Jumaily, in his white military uniform, deftly danced toward a long food-laden feast table. Half-dressed dark-haired women surrounded him as he picked from the plates of the sumptuous meal in a palace ballroom. Muscular soldiers meant to look like Americans in desert camouflage stood guard over Jumaily, who portrayed Iraq's new leader.

Jumaily smiled and waved from his palace chair. He cradled a large bottle of Johnny Walker whisky and grinned with pleasure. He sipped the expensive liquid from a crystal glass, toasting the air, while an old woman in a head scarf brought before him was dragged away by two "American soldiers."

The images accompanying the final stanzas of the theme song showed crowds of Iraqis running toward open-backed trucks. Men, women, and children jumped on board, waving white flags as the vehicles stirred up the dust departing into the desert, a comic symbol of the tragic mass exodus of Iraqis heading toward the border. The music changed to a familiar, ironic theme, an adult male chorus singing the opening refrain of the Arabic version of *Sesame Street*.

When *Selling the Country* was broadcast in September 2007, it was an instant hit inside Iraq and within the Iraqi exile community across the region, especially among the Sunnis. Wherever I went to interview Iraqi refugees, the television often was tuned to Al Sharqiya for another episode. The program broke old taboos because nothing was off-limits. In one episode, "Unlimited Stealing," the prime minister, concerned because of reports that his ministers were stealing money intended for development projects, decided to dedicate a new project himself. When he arrived at the building site there was no actual building, only a ceremonial band and the red tape to cut.

In another episode titled "Electricity," a reporter from the fictional "Electricity Television Channel" was arrested for asking why Iraqis must wait ten years for dependable power. The plot involved a failed plan by the government to build the largest generator in the world to run on bottled water rather than diesel fuel (easily available in oil-rich Iraq). It was like *Seinfeld* with a hard-core political message.

Iraqis knew firsthand about the failures of the new government. They lived with the consequences every day. The broadcast captured Iraq's attention because the scripts were laden with inside jokes and visual humor that came from an awareness of the daily depredations in Iraq, a deep knowledge of Iraqi culture and traditions, and a total disrespect for the new powers in Baghdad.

The reaction at the highest levels of government to the irreverence of *Selling the Country* could have been foretold. The cast would all get a hard lesson that criticism in the new Iraq would be tolerated no more than it had been in the old one.

The actors should have paid attention to the experience of Saad Khalifa, another Iraqi actor in Damascus who had performed in an earlier provocative political comedy broadcast into Iraq. Khalifa lived in a basement apartment in Yarmouk, a district of concrete homes, narrow streets, and cheap rents. He knew about the cost of dissent even from the safe haven of his small Damascus apartment.

The front room of Khalifa's house was the only one with any furniture. The others, visible from my perch on the flowered couch, were bare except for sleeping mats on the floor. Khalifa was well known inside and outside Iraq; his big face with the shadow of a graying beard was topped by a mop of curly salt-and-pepper hair. His large feet, in plastic flip flops, dangled from the overstuffed chair. Less than five feet tall, Khalifa was famously short. In person, his smallness, used as a comic trait on stage, leant him an air of sadness and vulnerability.

He had been the star of one of the most popular programs on Al Sharqiya. The title of the program, he told me, was the inoffensive Arabic label *Al Hukumat,* which means "The Government." But in a sly send-up that is possible in Arabic when the emphasis on the syllables is changed slightly, the title becomes *Hurry Up, He's Dead,* a play on words that reflected the conceit of the show that the central character is the last Iraqi left alive. The real death threats appeared as text messages on his cellphone a few weeks after the program aired.

"I don't know how long these threats last," said Khalifa, lighting another Gauloise cigarette as he recounted his fear in those first few days after the program aired. "It was officials in the government. The messages said, in a threatening way, why are you talking about the Iraqi government like this? Don't come back to Iraq!"

It was clear that whoever was delivering the threats knew how to track him down, even in exile. Khalifa's sense of safety was shattered:

"A singer, an old friend, who was close to the government, he also sent me a text message, 'Don't come back to Iraq!'" The messages were upsetting in themselves but raised a more troubling question: Was he safe even in Syria?

Khalifa served strong sugary tea in small glass cups. I noticed that his tracksuit pants had been crudely hand-stitched to mend the holes. Khalifa told me that his wife and son had left him and returned to Iraq, worn out by the uncertainty of the death threats and a life in exile.

His starring role in *Hurry Up, He's Dead* had poked fun at sectarianism, Saddam, and Iraq's new leaders. The program's theme song, about a cat, and the accompanying hip-hop-style music video, with Khalifa seated in a white stretch limousine, wearing star-shaped sunglasses and large curly wig, had prompted the death threats.

The "Cat Song," as it came to be known, was a direct assault on the new religious and sectarian identity of Iraq. Khalifa had made the song famous but he hadn't written the lyrics. The author, a writer and a journalist, wrote the song after narrowly escaping from a Shiite militia checkpoint in Baghdad near his home. The writer had been stopped and beaten up because he was obviously drunk.

He was tired and upset and on the way to his house he saw a cat and wondered, "Why am I not like this cat?" Nobody asks a cat where she comes from and nobody asks a cat whether she's Sunni or Shiite. A cat doesn't have to wear a business suit to a meeting. So he wrote the song from this viewpoint of the cat.

The "Cat Song," which became a music video played repeatedly on Arabic satellite channels and on YouTube, made Saad Khalifa a very famous man indeed. Many Iraqi exiles downloaded the tune and used it as a ringtone on their cellphones. Khalifa's performance was imitated by Iraqi children inside and outside of Iraq. He was featured in a glossy British magazine that profiled successful Muslims around the globe.

But despite his new international reputation, after everything he had been through, he insisted that he was sure he'd never take that kind of risk again.

"I have to consider my family, and also, whatever we say, nothing will change in Iraq. I was offered another political character in a production in Damascus, but I refused; it would be hard for me. We always hear in the news the words *democratic Iraq*, but a lot of people from our government are upset because we are using freedom to show what's happening there."

Selling the Country was the satirical successor to *Hurry Up, He's Dead*. By the time of the broadcast, Iraq's civil war had been settled in favor of the Shiites, and the Iraqi government had tightened its control on dissent, especially from Sunnis. But the government was fragile, panicky, and in no condition to tolerate being satirized.

Even before *Selling the Country* aired, militant Islamist websites posted the names of the entire cast and targeted them for death. One read, "We want to punish them and take revenge for all Iraqis. I know they will die faster than anything. God has to know they are bad people."

The threat was intensified when Iraq's prime minister, Nouri al-Maliki, made his first historic visit to Damascus in 2007. He handed Syria's President Bashar al-Assad a list of sixty-five names, all of them Iraqi actors and writers based in Damascus, and demanded their arrest. "This is a well-known story," Ahmed al-Akeedy told me wearily when we met later. The Syrian president turned down the arrest request. He was willing to protect a group of dissident Iraqi actors—a gesture he was unlikely to make for Syrian dissidents.

Zuhair Rasheed, the actor who played the prime minister, had already lost his brother and one of his sons, both killed in Iraq. When the threats began, he signed up with the United Nations High Commissioner for Refugees (UNHCR) office in Damascus and was quickly accepted for resettlement in Finland. Mace Gomar, the leading lady of the cast, was also targeted for harassment. Iraqis with close ties to the government came to Damascus to warn her not to go back. They levied an additional punishment, warning that her application for a new Iraqi passport would be rejected. Without a valid passport, she could not leave Syria even if she had been accepted for resettlement in another country.

The oversized Rasim al-Jumaily's health deteriorated rapidly in the months following the Ramadan broadcast of *Selling the Country*. He was the star of the show; his masterful comic performance as the new Iraqi leader had been one of the best in his long career. In December 2007, he collapsed, and his friend Ahmed al-Akeedy hurried him to a Damascus hospital on a cold winter night. Akeedy was certain that "this was the result of the pressure. We got the threats by text message. Jumaily's family in Baghdad was told, 'He can't come back, and he's a wanted man.'" Jumaily died after lingering in a coma for two days. Rumors swirled through the Iraqi actors' community in Damascus that Jumaily had been poisoned, that an Iraqi government hit squad had finally arrived to kill them all. Most of them hid at home for days after his death, terrified that they, too, were on an execution list.

What happened next went some way toward calming their fears and also surprised them. A day after Jumaily died, Iraqi government officials in Baghdad publicly embraced him as one of Iraq's most popular figures. Iraq's president, Jalal Talabani, whom Jumaily had most resembled in the television production, sent a telegram of condolences to Jumaily's family in Baghdad. In his message, released to the state-controlled media, Talabani called Jumaily "one of the Iraqi art flags for nearly a half century," and went on to say that "he has left a permanent place inside the hearts of all Iraqis through his work in theaters, cinema and TV." Had the Iraqi government accepted the criticisms of *Selling the Country*? Was this a sign that the culture war was over and satire could return to Iraq? In an official announcement, the Iraqi government pledged to "cover the cost of transporting the body of the deceased to Baghdad for burial in the homeland." The Iraqi government seemed to be welcoming Jumaily, if not his satire, home.

But the official plane never arrived to pick up his body. After five days, the community of actors and the family of Rasim al-Jumaily could wait no longer. "We kept Jumaily in a fridge in a Damascus hospital for five days. In Islam, you are supposed to bury them as soon as possible so the soul can rest." Akeedy recounted the events of the funeral, and bitterness swept over him again as he remembered the day in December 2007 when Iraq's exiled artistic community gathered in the outskirts of Damascus to bury Rasim al-Jumaily in a place called "The Strangers' Graveyard."

Akeedy had documented the funeral on a small hand-held camera. The black and white images began at the back door of the hospital as some in the Iraqi actor's community wheeled out a man-sized refrigerator where Jumaily's body had been kept. I could see a wooden coffin draped in an Iraqi flag tied onto the top of a car parked outside the hospital. A poster-sized picture of Jumaily, as a much younger man before the toll of exile had aged him, was framed over the coffin.

I watched the sharp images of the pallbearers as they opened the lid of the metal storage locker and lifted out a beige body bag. Akeedy told me they had discovered that the hospital staff had neglected to turn on the refrigerator for five days. The pallbearers grimaced at the smell, trying not to gag, as they hoisted their stiffened friend out of the white metal box. They struggled to carry the body bag toward the car and gently settled Jumaily into his coffin.

I could see that more than one hundred Iraqis—actors, directors, comedians—had gathered at the back entrance of the hospital to pay their last respects. They stood silently, watching the body being hoisted to the car roof. When the lid was closed they began a low

chant, "Pray for his soul" and "Rasim Jumaily is a good person," as the
pallbearers got into the long line of cars so the procession could get
under way.

The funeral motorcade was attended by the most famous Iraqi
artists exiled in Syria, and the caravan drove the coffin through neighborhoods where Iraqi exiles overwhelmingly outnumbered Syrians.
Thousands of Iraqis, Sunnis and Shiites, had lined the streets. The
traffic islands had black banners describing Middle Eastern fatalism,
"Death is God's right."

As Jumaily's coffin was lowered into the ground, Akeedy said, "All
of us were happy he was buried here. Iraqi television producers paid to
bury him and the Iraqi artists' association saved some money and gave
it to his family." Akeedy seemed pleased that this new community,
formed in exile, could rally and spare this famous Iraqi family the humiliation of a lonely funeral. The gathering seemed a celebration of the
old ways of Baghdad. Iraqi artists had come together to honor a man
who had a long career during the most perilous period of Iraqi history.
They had wanted to believe that their new government would embrace
them again, readmitting the spirit of mischievous theater that Rasim
al-Jumaily embodied and that was so much a part of the region's traditions and culture. But the government had failed, even humiliated, Jumaily, who would remain forever in Syrian soil. As they gathered at
Rasim al-Jumaily's graveside on a cold winter day, many of Iraq's most
famous artists had to wonder if they, too, would die far from home.

His triumph and theirs would come later, as the exiled actors in
Syria earned a living performing popular satires broadcast into Iraq
during Ramadan seasons to ever larger audiences each year. The 2009
hit *Who Wants to Win the Oil?* was a takeoff on *Who Wants to Be a
Millionaire?*, but in the Iraqi version contestants were played by well-
known comedians who competed to win a five-liter can of crude.
While freedom of expression was a consolation, it was certainly not
free, and Al Sharqiya, still considered the "Sunni channel," and reviled
by Iraqi government officials, remained in exile.

CHAPTER TWO

THE FIRST TO GO

In Damascus, the piano player in the decorated lobby of the Four Seasons hotel began his repertoire of Christmas melodies around lunchtime and ended sometime after midnight. Christmas trees twinkled in the shopping malls. Festive lights glimmered across balconies in the Muslim neighborhoods, a recent custom borrowed from Christian celebrations. Every thirty-three years, the major Christian and Muslim holidays of Christmas and Eid al-Adha fall close together. Christmas focuses on the birth of Jesus Christ; Eid al-Adha centers on Abraham, a shared prophet from the Koran and the Bible's Old Testament. December 2007 was one of those years of shared celebration. Secular, business-minded Damascus was a merry, decorated place preparing for family feasts. But for Iraqi exiles, especially the Christian community, the holiday season was a dispiriting time.

The collapse of multicultural Iraq had begun with the Christians. The first indications of the politics of displacement came not with the Sunnis but with the oldest community in Iraq, the Christians: Their experience of persecution, which began almost immediately after the U.S. invasion, was a model for the much larger Sunni crisis that would follow.

A recorded version of "White Christmas" was playing through the open door of a tourist trinket shop as I crossed the street and made my way into the sprawling compound of the Ibrahim Khalil Church in the Jeremana neighborhood of Damascus on a bright winter day. The church, the most impressive structure in an otherwise poor quarter of the capital, was a meeting place for Syria's Christian community on Sundays and during the week offered religious instruction programs for children. Syria's Christians, a minority in the country, are a confident community. New churches are built; the government paves the paths to ancient monasteries. Crosses are worn in plain sight. Syria's Christians have a tacit political alliance with a powerful Muslim minority, the Alawites, who have ruled the country since the late Hafez al-Assad seized power in 1970. This was a particularly Syrian sectarian formula to balance Syria's Sunni majority.

Syria's Christian churches welcomed Christians from Iraq when they were forced into exile, supporting them and integrating them into Christian neighborhoods. Unlike Baathist Syria, the Christian experience in Baathist Iraq had been harsh under Saddam and impossible during the sectarian warfare ignited by the American invasion.

Many Iraqi Christians had supported that invasion and hoped life might improve for them with the collapse of the Baath regime. But with the rise of militant Islam in Iraq, Christians were more directly associated with the hated West and therefore linked to the American presence. They became particular targets. It did not help that the muscular American evangelical movement arrived in Iraq along with American tanks. Samaritan's Purse, the global relief organization led by the Reverend Franklin Graham, who called Islam an "evil and wicked" religion, mobilized missionaries and relief supplies in the months after the invasion, which in turn mobilized militant Islamists to target Iraqi Christians.

As a result, Iraq's Christians were among the first to leave after Saddam's deposition. Their departure was the beginning of the cleansing of Iraq's historically diverse sectarian landscape. Some of the wealthiest Christian families crossed the borders within months of the arrival of American troops, and even more packed up after churches across the country were firebombed in coordinated attacks in 2004. Iraq's Christian exiles expected to qualify more easily for resettlement in the West and they could count on temporary shelter in the established Christian communities in the Middle East, in Lebanon, Jordan, and Syria.

But the resettlement process was agonizingly slow and the long wait was taking a toll. On a winter morning in Damascus, the basement kitchen of Ibrahim Khalil Church had been turned into a feeding center for Iraqi Christians sliding into destitution. Three times a week, stern Syrian nuns in stiff white habits ladled out fragrant lamb and rice from large aluminum pots. The church also opened a free medical clinic with volunteer Syrian doctors who doled out medicine for many chronically ill Iraqis who could no longer afford private care. Counseling for the vast number of rape cases and services for trauma victims, especially children, were very limited, but these were the only services available.

More than a hundred bedraggled Iraqis, most of them women, silently inched up the food line, their pans and plastic containers ready for a hot handout that was a welcome addition to a survival diet of bread and heavily sugared tea. Some told me, quietly, that their husbands had worked as translators for the U.S. military and had to leave the country when the family was threatened by neighborhood militias. They had packed quickly. Most said they had exhausted the family savings and now depended on food handouts. Muslims were welcome

here, too. The common denominators were hunger and humiliation
for people who had been part of Baghdad's middle class, which had
considered itself the Arab world's urban elite.

A few blocks away, in a sparsely furnished apartment, Nabras
Naseer, a rail-thin eighteen-year-old, sat alone for most of the day.
Naseer lived with his uncle's family in Damascus. The apartment, a
fourth-floor walk-up, looked like the temporary home they had hoped
it would be. The scant decorations included a couple of pictures of
Jesus, a green plastic vine that snaked across one wall, and a variety of
stuffed children's toys surrounding the television set.

Naseer, his dark hair parted down the middle, long enough to spill
over his delicate shoulders, his long face betraying no emotion, recounted his flight from Iraq in 2006, after spending ten days in a Baghdad hospital for traumatic injuries due to severe beatings.

He had wanted to be a computer engineer and was applying to
M'aamoon University in the Mansour neighborhood in Baghdad. He
left home early each morning so he could fill out applications for the
fall semester. He had been watched for days and had come under suspicion because the only employers in the country that required regular
hours were the U.S. forces and the Iraqi government.

"The reason behind kidnapping me, as they said, 'You are working
with the Americans.' There was no reason for them to think this, but
what they said was, 'You are a young guy, you leave your house every
morning at 7 A.M. and come back at a regular time in the afternoon.
Where are you spending your time? So you must be working for the
Americans.'"

"What they said was, 'We are going to investigate you, and if we
find out that you were working for the Americans, then we will cut
your head off.'"

It was early afternoon as we talked, and the sound of children returning from school filled the hallway of the apartment building, but

Naseer seemed unaware of his surroundings. He started to speak again, but when the doorbell rang a second time, he heaved himself out of the chair to open the door for a small boy weighed down with a backpack full of schoolbooks. "My nephew," said Naseer, without a smile.

I asked Naseer if he wanted his young nephew to hear the rest of story. Dismissing what he seemed to consider my misplaced sensitivity, he said, "His cousin was kidnapped, and we don't know anything about him." However gruesome his own ordeal, at least he was alive to tell it. That made it suitable for an eight-year-old boy's ears. A framed wedding picture of the boy's cousin, an image from happier family times, hung beneath a decorative clock that had stopped.

Naseer's family home had been in the Iraqi neighborhood of Dura, a mixed neighborhood sometimes known as "The Vatican," in acknowledgment of the large number of Christians who lived there. The Christian community has ancient roots in Iraq, but life under Saddam's regime had been difficult from the start. In 1974, Saddam abolished nongovernment schools, closing thirty-four Christian educational institutions including the Jesuit College in Baghdad that had schooled the capital's Muslim elite. However, under Saddam, Iraqi Christians were free to worship in neighborhood churches and there were business opportunities that were off-limits for Muslims. In secular Iraq, Christians could sell gold and alcohol. They did a brisk business in a country that considered *arak* the national drink and a necessary part of the evening meal.

By the time of Nabras Naseer's kidnapping in 2006, a group called "Al Qaeda in Mesopotamia" ruled his neighborhood, terrorizing civilians, Christians and Shiites alike. Dura was prime real estate for insurgents and militias, a much-fought-over few miles that changed hands from one brutal group to another. The location, next to a major highway, afforded a quick escape from security forces. Many houses in the neighborhood were large and comfortable, roomy enough for makeshift prisons, and the vast farmland nearby was ideal for stashing weapons, and discarding bodies.

The kidnappers, young men in civilian clothes, seized Naseer as he returned home from the university, roughly bundling him into the trunk of a car. "It all happened in ten minutes," he said. "Not one of them looked familiar, but they were speaking an Iraqi dialect," meaning that the kidnappers were local Sunni men, not Arabs from other countries who had come to wage jihad in Iraq.

Naseer was taken to a house in the Dura neighborhood where he was shoved into a room with six other terrified Iraqi men and an eleven-year-old boy.

"They took all of my things, including my cellphone, and told me they were taking me to a trial," Naseer told me. His hand brushed his neck.

Within hours of his capture, the kidnappers called his parents from the home number on his cellphone. This was often the pattern whether kidnappers intended to kill their victim or not. Violence in Iraq sometimes involved a personal relationship between the kidnappers and the victim's family, one side pleading, the other side taunting, in negotiations over ransom or the location of a body. "They told my mom, 'We will cut his head off if we find out he was working for the Americans.' My mother couldn't handle the shock so she collapsed," Naseer said.

Naseer's father picked up the phone to speak to the kidnappers, and his quick thinking may ultimately have saved his son's life.

"They told the same story to my dad and then my dad told them, 'If you find any documents that say he works for the Americans, then I will cut his head off myself.'"

Naseer spoke of the days and nights in prison in a passionless voice. "They would show me a photo of Zarqawi on a cellphone. 'Who is this?' We would say Zarqawi. 'No, you have to say this is Molana, Our Lord. If you didn't say that they would beat you.'"

Almost every Iraqi could recognize a picture of Abu Musab al-Zarqawi, the Jordanian militant Islamist who led the most violent wing of Al Qaeda in Mesopotamia. He had promoted indiscriminate attacks on Iraqi civilians he considered "non-believers," who, in his extreme ideology, included all non-Muslims, as well as Iraq's Shiites. Zarqawi had died in a U.S. airstrike in June 2006, but his death made no difference to his young Iraqi followers who had sworn allegiance to his ideology and to the wider movement of an Islamist jihad against the West and anyone or anything associated with the hated Americans. For them, Al Qaeda offered clear, concrete answers in a confusing and unjust Iraq.

"They were telling me, 'This is not just about working for the Americans. You are a Christian and you do not have a place in Iraq.' They were cursing Christians and they said Christians were full of sin. 'Iraq is not your place.'"

Al Qaeda in Mesopotamia introduced beheading to the already extensive Iraqi vocabulary of violence. The first execution was documented and released a month after the Abu Ghraib prison scandal became public in 2004. Abu Musab al-Zarqawi had recorded the execution of Nicolas Berg, a twenty-six-year-old American civilian. The images of Berg in his orange jumpsuit, similar to those worn by the accused held at the U.S. detention facility in Guantanamo Bay, Cuba, had become a recruitment tool as well as a tutorial. Young Iraqi men told me that they collected beheading videos, downloading them to computers when the electricity worked, or storing the images on cellphones to share with others.

Naseer said he witnessed three separate beheadings over the next eleven days, including the death of the eleven-year-old boy who finally "confessed" to his kidnappers that he had told U.S. soldiers the locations of roadside bombs in his neighborhood. Naseer was forced by his captors to witness these beheadings. But these young Iraqis who claimed to be part of Al Qaeda in Mesopotamia were unschooled in the technique of quickly ending life with a strategic swipe of a sharp knife across the major neck artery. They failed to find that crucial spot. The executioners forced the condemned to drink some kind of caustic liquid to subdue them before delivering a long, brutal, and grisly end.

Naseer's story is no more gruesome than other exiles' experience. But it is symptomatic of the damage inflicted on hundreds of thousands of Iraqis by other Iraqis.

UNHCR, the United Nations' refugee agency, tried to quantify the human damage in a study conducted in conjunction with the Center for Disease Control in Atlanta. The polling data showed that the vast majority of exiles suffered from depression and anxiety. More than 60 percent said they experienced symptoms of post-traumatic stress disorder. Most were in deep emotional despair, far more so, according to the study, than refugees from any other recent conflicts. The statistics revealed that an extraordinary number of exiles had experienced violence firsthand.

According to the data, 77 percent of respondents had been affected by air bombardments, shelling, or rocket attacks; 80 percent had witnessed a shooting; 68 percent had undergone interrogation or harassment by militias; and 75 percent knew someone close to them who had been killed.

In Iraq, the targeting of victims had a horrific logic in a zero-sum game where "sectarian cleansing" was employed to assert a new Iraqi identity—an identity based on sectarian allegiances that Saddam's regime had submerged. The death squads frequently operated in the same territory with overlapping and often-competing ideologies. The death lists were more complex than the sectarian divide. Entire professional classes were targeted for death: doctors, teachers, computer technicians, professors. Even barbers and bakers were at risk because of their alleged "anti-Islamic" practices. Former Baathists were targeted from the beginning, along with high-ranking army officers and air force pilots who had fought in the Iran-Iraq war.

Over time, the death lists came to include secularists, couples in mixed marriages, alcohol drinkers, soccer players who wore shorts on the playing field, and even Iraqis who used ice cubes or ate *samoon* bread, the leavened football-shaped loaf unique to Iraqi cuisine. The bread was prohibited by the Sunni extremists who argued that the Prophet Muhammad did not eat *samoon*. The Al Qaeda jihadists invented rules, banned anything not in use during the Prophet Muhammad's time, and passed life and death judgments that were as ludicrous as they were brutal and immoral. "They even killed female goats because their private parts were not covered and their tails were pointed upward, which they said was *haram* [forbidden]," said an Iraqi who was forced to comply or be killed. "They regarded the cucumber as male and the tomato as female. Women were not allowed to buy cucumbers!"

Women were particular targets in general; those who would not wear the black *abaya* (the all-enveloping cloak of Islamic modesty), and even those who did but wore makeup or lipstick, were considered to be showing defiance against the new rules imposed by militant Islamists inside and outside the government.

By 2005, Iraqis were dying violently in staggering numbers. How many deaths became a charged political argument. In 2006, the *New England Journal of Medicine* entered the debate with a study showing that violence was the *leading* cause of death for all Iraqi adults and the *main* cause of death for men between fifteen and fifty-nine years of age. The Sunni insurgency's alliance with Al Qaeda began with the common goal of fighting the U.S. occupation, but Al Qaeda's brutal tactics, massacring Shiite civilians and targeting Shiite religious institutions, would eventually drag the entire Sunni community into a confrontation with the better-equipped Shiite militias backed by Ministry of Interior forces.

Nabras Naseer, in the basement prison cell in Dura, disoriented and half-mad from his ordeal, was ruled innocent of working with the Americans by his Sunni captors, but still guilty of being a Christian. His family was required to pay a $30,000-dollar ransom—a "tax" on Christians—to gain his release. He was freed a few miles from his home after thirteen days in captivity:

> When they released me I was in a hurry to get to my home in Dura. They could not open one of the chains on my hands so I still had handcuffs on when I waved down a taxi. I put both of my hands in my pockets so the driver couldn't see that I had been a prisoner. We were about to arrive in front of my house, and the driver turned to me and said, "Please, son, I am a man with a family; don't blow yourself up in my taxi."
>
> I took out my hands and told him what had happened to me. He believed me, that I was not a suicide bomber. He was so relieved that he didn't ask me to pay anything for the ride home.

But Naseer was still disoriented from the deprivations of his imprisonment and the two weeks of beatings by his local Al Qaeda jailers, so his parents brought him to a neighborhood hospital for treatment. They arranged for him to leave the country as soon as he was well enough to travel and live with relatives already in exile in Damascus.

Iraq's Christians make up at least 15 percent of those who have fled the country, a stunning number considering that Christians accounted for only about 3 percent of the pre-invasion population. Across the country, Al Qaeda of Mesopotamia carried out the vicious targeted campaign to drive them out, convert them, or kill them. The militants imposed a tax—the *jizya*, or protection money—and compelled Christian women to wear the *hijab*. Christians suffered from coerced conversions to Islam, including demands to hand over daughters in marriage to consummate the forced acceptance of the Islamic faith. For those who refused, the punishments were severe: rape, torture, murder, as well as the destruction of their homes.

Many of Baghdad's Christians left the country but some also escaped to Mosul, a provincial capital with a population of more than one million people. Mosul was considered a sanctuary because the city was a traditional melting pot for all of Iraq's major sects and ethnic groups. This second-largest city in Iraq also had historical resonance because it claimed one of the oldest Christian communities in the world. Across the Tigris River was the ancient Assyrian capital city of Nineveh. The once powerful Assyrian empire was the first nation to accept Christianity; the first church was founded by St. Thomas.

But even in Mosul, Christians could not escape the danger. The city had come under the murderous sectarian logic that was tearing the rest of Iraq apart. The Sunni Arabs, a minority in the capital, were the dominant sectarian group in Mosul, but the Kurds were in charge of the local administration after winning in elections when the Sunnis opted out of the vote. The Christians, lacking a militia of their own, were caught in the middle of a power struggle for control of Mosul and neighboring Kirkuk. When Al Qaeda groups were added to this volatile mix the Christian community suffered repeated waves of violence.

As the U.S. surge got under way in Baghdad, squeezing out Al Qaeda groups from the capital, many Islamic militants headed north, regrouping in Mosul, turning the city into the last urban stronghold for the insurgency in Iraq. In 2008, the violent campaign against the Christian community accelerated.

Fear spiked in February with a high-profile kidnapping and murder. The Chaldean Catholic Archbishop Paulos Faraj Rahho was abducted after leading the prayers at the Church of the Holy Spirit. Three people with him at the time—a driver and two guards—were killed by the kidnappers, and the defenseless archbishop was bundled into the trunk of a car. Remarkably, in the dark, alone for probably the last time until his death, the sixty-five-year-old archbishop managed to get out his last cellphone call. He was determined to deliver a final message to his congregation, instructions that would ensure he would never be released alive. He begged them *not* to pay any ransom for his life. He knew from bitter experience how futile such payoffs were: Archbishop Rahho had been making them for years.

It is not clear when the archbishop began to hand over the alms he collected at Sunday mass to the Sunni militants who menaced his congregation. The details emerged only after his death. The men who had come to him said they were with Al Qaeda and demanded *jizya*, protection money. It is a tax as old as Islam, levied on Christian and Jews. But in the modern context of Mosul, it was administered like a mafia shakedown. Archbishop Rahho paid for protection he didn't get. The militants continued to kidnap priests, demanding thousands of dollars in ransom and victimizing the community even as the Christians of Mosul continued to pay. The payments were financing the militants who were killing them. Christians were digging into their life savings and sweetening the money pot with thousands more dollars in international donations. The archbishop must have been convinced that if he didn't pay, the violence would have been much worse.

A month before he was abducted, Rahho appeared on local television denouncing the protection racket. Although it didn't seem so at the time, this was a declaration directed at the Islamic militants. He was declaring that he had finished funding a campaign that was leading to the slow extinction of the Christians of Iraq. Perhaps mistaking the relatively calm situation in Baghdad after the surge as a sign that peace was possible, and not just a temporary cessation of hostilities because neighborhoods had been ethnically cleansed, Rahho must have decided that the security gains were permanent and that as the Americans applied the same strategy in Mosul he would no longer have to pay for "protection." He finally decided to call a halt to a system that was supporting death squads.

When the bag-man came to the church for the usual payment, Rahho turned him down. But the archbishop's death raised a number of issues that would become part of the calculations when Iraqi Christians in exile weighed the decision to return. Why hadn't the Iraqi government done more to protect the community in the capital and in Mosul? Why hadn't government ministers spoken out against the victimization? Could the Christians of Mosul trust Kurdish officials who had their own agenda and were trying to gain political dominance in the districts of Nineveh province, often at the expense of the Christians? How could a minority community join in building the future of the country as long as the political system was defined on the basis of sectarian identity?

Some Iraqi Christians came back in 2009 to check out Iraqi government and U.S. claims of improved security and living conditions, but they didn't stay long. In Baghdad, it was still dangerous to reclaim a house that had been taken over by another sectarian group. Security was improving and Al Qaeda has been substantially weakened, but not completely defeated. The horrific murders specifically targeting Christians were rare. But for many in Iraq's middle class, security was not the only consideration.

The prime minister, Nouri al-Maliki, made an important gesture, urging Christians to come home after a meeting with Pope Benedict XVI in Rome in July 2008. The Vatican was the stage for the symbolic appearance. Christians around the world had been sounding the alarm that Christians in Iraq faced extinction. Maliki said he needed the skills of such an educated minority to rebuild the battered country. He urged the pontiff to encourage Christians to return to build a new future. But at home, the prime minister supported an ethno-sectarian quota system known as *muhasasa*, which governed job opportunities in every ministry and dictated the distribution of important government posts. The quota system dictated the number of seats on provincial government councils. Merit and educational achievement were not enough for a successful job application. Sectarian identity was the basis for government policy. Maliki wanted the return of the skilled middle class, but his quota system was no meritocracy: It rewarded the biggest religious factions—and that was all. The political divide in Iraq was as wide as ever. After the surge, the Americans were talking of drawing down and leaving. Security had improved, but the surge had failed to leverage the security success into the political reconciliation that was necessary for a stable Iraq.

There was no sign that Iraq's politicians were able or willing to make the necessary compromises to develop a government of national unity. The fault lines in Iraq could erupt into violence again, plunging the Christian community back into the middle of a power struggle. In the spring of 2009, the European Union offered a solution for some in the exile community by offering to resettle ten thousand refugees. By giving priority to persecuted minorities, Europe finally opened its doors to thousands of Christian families from Iraq. The German newspaper *Die Welt* highlighted the paradox of the resettlement:

> When we as Christians take in Christians living under a permanent state of threat in Iraq, we, in effect, give in to radical powers which aim to turn Iraq into a Christian-free zone. Naturally, it would be much better if the Christians, who have a 2,000-year history in the country, were secured a future in the region. It would be a defeat if

the final third of the once 800,000-strong Christian community were displaced.

Jamal Arafat, a United Nations official with UNHCR based in Jordan, was appalled by Europe's deliberately sectarian resettlement policy. "It started with the French," he told me in August 2009, "then the Germans, and now the Swedes. Sweden is blatantly rejecting non-Christians from Iraq."

Yet the defeat seemed inevitable. Another civilizational and cultural strand of old Iraq had been unwound and cast aside. The Christians would have to make their futures elsewhere, it seemed.

CHAPTER THREE

SURGE OF EXILE

Syria closed the border and blocked further mass emigration from Iraq in October 2007, but Iraqi exiles in Damascus had no doubt who was to blame. They muttered darkly about Nouri al-Maliki, Iraq's prime minister. Many exiles were convinced that Maliki—under pressure from Washington because the outflow of Iraqis was an embarrassing counter to the rhetoric of progress—had persuaded the Syrians to shut the last open door. "He wants to convince the world that Iraq is stable, that his government is a success," said one Iraqi refugee. "We cannot go back. They will kill us all!"

Prime Minister Maliki personally took the hardest line within the Iraqi government against the exiles. Syrian officials were shocked when, during his visit, they heard Maliki call the exiles "cowards" and showed little concern for the welfare of more than two million Iraqis who had been forced out of the country. Under American pressure, Maliki's government had grudgingly pledged $25 million to Jordan and Syria to help subsidize the costs of hosting the exile Iraqi population, but did not deliver the cash for eighteen. The prime minister's office vetoed a plan by the Iraqi Red Crescent to truck food rations across the border to the neediest exile population. The exiled Iraqis took the neglect personally. They believed the government had abandoned them. They believed their desperate circumstances were a source of national shame at a time when the Iraqi government coffers were filling up again with oil profits. In Baghdad, as well as in Washington, it was politically preferable to pretend the causes that led to their exile didn't exist.

After October 2007, Syria's new, restricted visa regime permitted only academics, merchants with established business ties in Syria, and taxi and truck drivers to cross the border. Iraqis had to apply for visas at the Syrian embassy in Baghdad, which was in a dangerous neighborhood. In the last week leading up to the Syrian closure, more than twenty thousand Iraqis streamed through the crossing at Al-Tanf every day. It was the last chance: The cars and buses formed a waiting line more than fifteen miles long. The majority of the exiles were Sunni Muslims.

Despite his publicly professed vision to unite Iraq's Sunnis, Shiites, and Kurds, Nouri al-Maliki's political leadership was based on his experience as the leader of an underground Shiite movement during Saddam's time. He distrusted a wide array of political players across Iraq's landscape, including Iraq's Sunni politicians and even Shiite insiders (both tribal and secular)—those who had not shared Maliki's decades in the underground fight against Saddam Hussein's regime. Maliki's strongly sectarian agenda would ultimately undermine the larger goals of a new U.S. security strategy for Iraq.

The two-part surge strategy in 2007 was simple and direct. As the extra American troops reduced the bloodshed in Iraq, Iraq's leaders would have the breathing room and confidence they needed, in Washington's view, to turn away from their militias and private armies.

Weakening Al Qaeda in Iraq would also reduce the power of the two major Shiite militias: Muqtada al-Sadr's Mahdi army and the Badr Corps, the military arm of the Islamic Supreme Council of Iraq. For protection, Shiite communities counted on the militias rather than on the Iraqi army, which they viewed as less motivated and ill-prepared to handle insurgents and terror attacks. As security improved, it was hoped that the perceived need for such militias would decline and a process of national reconciliation could begin. A grand bargain that settled the division of power between the Sunnis and Shiites of Iraq would ease the fundamental cause of sectarian violence. That was the plan, anyway.

Despite Prime Minister Maliki's pledges to work for political reconciliation, he was unable or unwilling to rein in the Shiite militias in the capital—in particular, Sadr's militia, the Jaysh al-Mahdi (known to the U.S. military as the JAM).

"The JAM saw certain neighborhoods as strategic and tactical," recalled Lieutenant Colonel Jeff Ragland, who worked at U.S. military headquarters in Baghdad. As additional U.S. troops spread across the capital, security began to improve and markets and parks reopened for the first time in years, but it took time to place thirty thousand soldiers in Baghdad's trouble spots. In pockets of the capital, particularly neighborhoods in the north and west, the Mahdi militia continued a relentless campaign to purge Sunnis from remaining mixed areas, a rush of last-minute unfinished business ahead of the full U.S. deployment of troops.

"We wanted to solve the problem and have everything done and have everybody singing kumbaya," Lieutenant Colonel Ragland told me. "But I had no expectations that we would be able to get there. It was in the too-hard-to-do box."

Jeff Ragland, and others, argued these misgivings to the commanders in Baghdad. For Ragland, this was his job. He had deployed as the commander of the first so-called Red Team that had served at U.S. military headquarters in the Iraqi capital. In military war gaming, the Red Team is known as the opposing force, tasked with revealing the weaknesses in military preparedness. This Red Team unit was part of a new and unusual program designed to break through the "group-think" that had led to the disastrous military policies in the first three years of the war. Ragland was among the first graduates trained to challenge conventional military thinking on the battlefield in a program at Fort Leavenworth's University of Foreign Military and Cultural Studies. One of his assignments in Baghdad was to continually question basic assumptions about the surge.

"I did have a discussion with the highest elements of the command over there. I said, 'Look, this is going to get transitory security, you can't help but get it. But I honestly think you are going to fail to get a lasting success.' I said, 'you will fail to achieve the mission you are trying to accomplish.'"

Throughout the spring and summer of 2007, Iraq's Sunnis and Shiites remained at war, and political reconciliation, at least on the neighborhood level, was not possible. Not even close.

By the fall of that year, the casualties for U.S. soldiers and violent attacks against Iraqis began to plummet. In November, Rear Admiral Gregory Smith, a U.S. military spokesman, declared the operation in Baghdad a success, with Iraqi civilian casualties down by 75 percent and violence across the country down by 60 percent.

But what were the reasons for the unprecedented and sudden drop in violence? The statistics for violent civilian deaths showed a dramatic increase through the summer, including the most car-bomb attacks in Iraqi history, but in September the trend sharply reversed. The key factors that led to the dramatic reversal remained hotly debated among diplomats, journalists, and military officers.

In August 2007, Muqtada al-Sadr declared a cease-fire, suspending the activities of his powerful Mahdi army. The "Awakening," the shorthand term for the Sunni tribal revolt against Al Qaeda in Mesopotamia, in alliance with U.S. forces, also helped to moderate violent attacks over time. Of course, the surge of American troops had certainly played an important role. But there was one other key factor being debated in Iraq and in the region. The sectarian landscape in the Iraqi capital had decisively shifted. Baghdad became a Shiite-dominated city for the first time in its long history. Communities were separated by religious identity and now lived behind protective blast walls, the physical sign of a psychological break. Many of the mixed neighborhoods that had been a feature of old Baghdad had been purged. Baghdad was calmer, the death counts continued to decline, but there was little debate about political progress. Separation along sectarian lines made reconciliation unimaginable.

In Douma, on the outskirts of the Syrian capital, the United Nations High Commissioner for Refugees had converted a warehouse into a refugee reception center north of Damascus to process the crowds of new exiles. There were hundreds of Iraqis in line every day with hours to wait and harrowing stories to tell. In Douma, the truth of what had happened in Baghdad, from which more than 80 percent of the new arrivals had come, was revealed.

The stories were tragic and familiar: A husband shot dead, a child kidnapped then killed. The gang rape of a daughter or a son, a note on the door that said "leave or die." There were endless savage permutations. I kept track of the neighborhoods the exiles had come from and made a mental map of the Iraqi capital. It was harder to ask "Sunni or Shiite?" Most of the Iraqis in line would have refused to answer my question, but the United Nations kept track because "religion" was part of the personal form they had to fill out. The new arrivals were mostly Sunnis.

Mohammed Yahya, an English-speaking veterinarian who for eighteen months had worked for a U.S. government contractor inside
Baghdad's Green Zone and then took a job as a translator for a British
news organization, lived in a building in which the Mahdi army had
set up a security office and was beginning to investigate the tenants.
Yahya found himself thinking of the many ways in which he
to die. He considered that he might be beheaded as a spy-
close to the Mahdi army had told him this had happene
working for the Americans—or, as Baghdad became mor
that he might be killed on the highway to central Baghda
home in Hurriyah, as it was often hit by roadside bomb
rattled the windows and shook his apartment. Hurriy
tested neighborhood in 2006. Al Qaeda in Iraq had moved in and
three snipers had set up a post in the Sunni mosque near his apartment building. Everywhere, Yahya was stalked by violent death.

Hurriyah, which means "Freedom," had been a mixed neighborhood where Sunni and Shiites lived together and married across sectarian lines during Saddam's time, but by 2007 many of Hurriyah's
Sunni residents had been driven out by the Mahdi militiamen and the
neighborhood had become almost entirely a Shiite enclave.

Yahya knew that the violent remnants of Al Qaeda in Iraq had finally been defeated when he saw three human heads in the garbage
dump near his home. The Sunni mosque was burned and broken.
New banners celebrating revered Shiite Imams appeared on neighborhood streets. The human heads remained atop the garbage dump
for days. Mohammed had to shield his children from the gruesome
sight when they ventured outside.

"Those heads belonged to the [Al Qaeda] snipers," he said flatly,
the dead snipers a sign that the neighborhood battle was over. The
Mahdi army victory meant Hurriyah was mostly quiet, but the daily
life of the residents was monitored and controlled by militiamen.

Soon, expulsions of the remaining Sunni families began. Yahya could draw back his curtains and see his neighbors on the curbside with small suitcases. "They weren't allowed to take much with them, just a few personal items. Sometimes they were forced to walk away from their homes with nothing." More than one hundred houses changed hands over the next few months.

A company of American soldiers had also set up a security station in the neighborhood, as a surge tactic, but the Iraqis of Hurriyah—the remaining Sunnis and Shiites alike—did not believe the Americans could protect them, not from the expulsions, nor from the Mahdi militia. The militiamen became the local government, controlling daily life by doling out gas and medicine in exchange for loyalty. The thugs-turned-real-estate-agents rented out the apartments they had emptied. Shiite families who had been expelled from other neighborhoods in Baghdad moved in. The new residents settled into new surroundings, fully furnished with other people's lives. Such rearrangements of sectarian groups had been taking place all over Baghdad. The coerced home swaps complicated any future mass-exile return. Who would untangle the housing claims for thousands of displaced Iraqis?

Safa Rasul Hussein was also watching events in Hurriyah, but from a somewhat safer post inside the Green Zone. During Saddam Hussein's rule, Safa Rasul had risen through the ranks of the Iraqi air force to the post of brigadier general and later worked as a director of a research and development center in the Military Industries Ministry. But even as he worked for Saddam, Safa Rasul, a high-ranking Shiite officer, had quietly kept channels open to Iraq's dissidents-in-exile. "I was in the underground; we were a handful who did so. I was not a complete stranger to the exiles when Saddam fell," he explained. In 2003, Safa Rasul was selected to join the Iraq Governing Council as a deputy minister. With his extensive knowledge of the country—more detailed and up-to-date than that of any of the exiles who had returned to

Iraq—Safa Rasul was chosen for a seat on the Iraqi government's National Security Council and became the deputy national security advisor. He observed firsthand the arrival of Iranian support for the Mahdi army.

This was one reason that the remaining Sunni families were purged from the neighborhood, Safa Rasul told me. There were other reasons.

"Imagine yourself a member of the Mahdi militia," he said, referring to a mental exercise he had often conducted himself as an analyst in the National Security Council. "You are committed to attacking the Americans and the Iraqi army. What you want is a safe area for your operations. So you target anyone you believe has a connection with the Americans or the Iraqi army." This was an intelligence operation, eliminating anyone who might pose a threat.

Safa Rasul, though a Shiite himself, was married to a Sunni. He was contemptuous of the Mahdi militia: "Now, they aren't competent in intelligence," he continued, describing the operations of the Shiite militia, "so they suspect all Sunnis. This is a division based on fear." For the militiamen, the safest course was to take no chances and to rid the neighborhood of all the Sunni families that remained. "These are not ideological or strategic decisions but, rather, local ones. They do this where they can. It is a human trend." Safa Rasul added another reason for the expulsions in Hurriyah and the other mixed neighborhoods of Baghdad: "They made a huge business renting apartments and competing among themselves." In essence, Baghdad's new sectarian map was also driven by the steady income of the real estate market.

The day Sadr's security officers installed themselves in one of the empty apartments in his building, Mohammed Yahya felt the danger of his secret life as a translator for Westerners in Iraq closing in. He packed lightly for the drive to Damascus, telling his neighbors he was taking the family on vacation in Syria now that the school year was over. He asked his neighbors to look after his apartment, then closed and locked the door. He said he would be back soon. Any departure was noted by the checkpoint guards and by the security officers who spent the day on the floor below. Yahya still had relatives in Baghdad and his secret life, if discovered, would put them at risk.

"Even here in Damascus, I don't tell people that I worked with the Americans, even here," Yahya said. "I know the Mahdi army is here in Damascus and they can hurt my family in Iraq. I have my parents back there."

He had rented an apartment in a neighborhood where Syrians lived rather than the cheaper places in the suburbs packed with refugees—better to avoid bumping into friends or enemies from home. Yahya said he felt safer in Damascus: He had learned to fall asleep in a city without gunfire at night. He walked the streets without constantly checking over his shoulder. But like most of the exiles, he was running out of savings. The rents in Damascus were going up; education for his oldest son was expensive. The war had exacted a high price on his family, too.

"My youngest son," he told me, "still has bad dreams and cries at night. He stutters sometimes and refuses to go to kindergarten. He insists he must stay home with his mother."

Most of all, Yahya worried about how long he could hold out in Damascus. There was no work, and day-to-day encounters with Syrians were increasingly strained as the crime rates and rents soared. Insistent rumors among the exile community suggested that the Syrian government would soon terminate residency for Iraqis. In the streets of Saida Zeinab, the quarters where many exiles had rented small cheap apartments, the cadence of Iraqi-accented Arabic and cassette players warbling prayers were often overwhelmed by the street hawkers shouting "Baghdad, Baghdad" and "Border, Border." These calls were a reminder that, to maintain a legal passport stamp, every ninety days Iraqis had to travel to the border, get an exit stamp, and then

reenter Syria. It was an expensive, exhausting trip, especially for families with children. But the exiles knew that—at any time—the Syrians could stop adding the stamp that allowed them back in.

All of these anxieties weighed on the exile community during the
August 2007 visit to Damascus by Prime Minister Maliki, the first
high-level Iraqi delegation to arrive since the two countries had restored diplomatic ties a year earlier after a twenty-year hiatus. During
Saddam's time, the enmity between Damascus and Baghdad was
stamped in Syrian passports, which allowed visits to "Arab countries
except Iraq." But the border had been open since 2003 and border
traffic was at the top of the agenda for relations between the two
countries.

In the new era, the Syrian welcome for Maliki and the Iraqi delegation was warm and red-carpet. It was Maliki's first trip abroad as
prime minister, and a personal homecoming to the city where he himself had been a political exile. From Damascus in the 1980s, Maliki
had helped organize financial networks abroad and guerrilla fighters
committed to slipping back over the border to try to weaken Saddam's
regime. Maliki knew firsthand the hardships of exile. He also knew
all too well that an exile community was a breeding ground for dissent
and underground organizations. In Damascus for more than a decade,
Maliki, an operative for Dawa, a conspiratorial underground Shiite
movement, had been Dawa's contact man with Syrian intelligence.

The aim of the high-profile Iraqi visit to Damascus was to formalize
a security deal with Syria. The agreement was intended to reinforce
the porous 466-mile border, which U.S. officials repeatedly insisted was
the crossing point for most of the foreign fighters who came to join Al
Qaeda in Iraq. Maliki told Syrian officials that the constant flow of
refugees was also a security threat. That's why he wanted the border
closed. Just as important, the constant flow of frightened Iraqis across
the Syrian border was a public embarrassment for his government.

With the border flows staunched, the Iraqi government seized on a plan to demonstrate progress to members of the U.S. Congress who were calling for Maliki's ouster. If some in the exile population began to head back to Baghdad, Maliki could claim the homecoming was proof that the new security plan was a success, a public relations victory.

In November 2007, signs went up in the refugee neighborhoods of Damascus offering a free bus ride and $800 to every family who agreed to go back to Iraq. Iraq's state television channel broadcast commercials that used soft-focus emotional vignettes to proclaim that safety had been restored. Government spokesman Ali al-Dabbagh said, "The Iraqi government is eager to have Iraqis return to their country and live a normal, safe life." But how eager?

On a sunny winter day, twenty buses, each with seats for about thirty extended families, filled quickly and headed southeast from Damascus. But the great return stalled as soon as the convoy crossed the border. The Syrian bus drivers did not have the proper documents to drive all the way to Baghdad. Passengers had to wait overnight, sleeping in the buses, while drivers from Baghdad headed out to pick them up. The convoy, protected by helicopter and police escort, proceeded slowly, arriving in the Iraqi capital more than forty-eight hours after the departure from Damascus on what was usually a fourteen-hour trip.

The exhausted returnees were greeted at a reception organized at a Baghdad hotel. A government minister, with great fanfare, handed over the promised payments. Television crews from around the world filmed the scene. But no one else was there to greet them because relatives had been mistakenly informed that the drop-off point was across town. Even so, the first government-financed bus trip—and as it happened, the only government-sponsored trip in 2007—had been a public relations success. Many commentators and politicians in the

United States hailed the return of the refugees; it was an unmistakable sign, they insisted, that the U.S. surge was a success. The television pictures of the returning families had proven it.

Weeks later it turned out that some of the returnees had been kidnapped as they left the reception, held up for the $800 government grant that they had in hand. Only a third of the families were able to move back to their original homes; the rest discovered that other families had moved in and would not move out, the refusal often made at gunpoint. Without any mechanism to settle property disputes, the returnees moved in with relatives or rented rooms in new neighborhoods—each family according to its sectarian identity. Some even headed back to Damascus, closed border or not.

The saga of the expensive bus trip was quickly relayed to the exile community in Damascus. Iraqis read about it on the Internet and discussed the details with relatives back home. They could also see a U.S. military spokesman's repeated interviews on Al Jazeera television saying that Baghdad was not yet ready for a mass influx of refugees because it would undermine the fragile security that had been established in the capital.

Back in Damascus, the Iraqi government had opened a dozen offices across the city at which Iraqis could sign up for the free bus rides home. A few weeks after the first convoy, I went to the Iraqi government office in Saida Zeinab to see if anyone was signing up. Fa'ak Sadi, a short, dapper man with a small metal map of Iraq pinned to the lapel of his wool suit, was in charge. I had arrived without an appointment, but Sadi warmly welcomed me into his office with a perfectly pronounced English sentence. "Welcome, glad to see you," he said, offering a hand to shake. But this was the limit of his English-language skills. He had spent time in the United States twenty-three years ago, he said in Arabic, and this was the one phrase he remembered.

"The issue of the buses is complicated," he told me slowly, as he gestured to another man in the room to bring us tea. "We were embarrassed because the government spokesman told people that these buses would leave every day," he continued when the tea had finally arrived.

When I asked if he thought the Iraqi government would continue the program by funding more bus trips, he left open the possibility with an unconvincing shrug of his shoulders. In the front room of the office, an Iraqi couple had completed a form to get on the list for the next bus. They had been the only customers all evening.

In the cold night air on the curbside in front of the government office, an Iraqi man in a worn tracksuit sat in a wheelchair behind a portable plastic table. He sold cellphone cards to a crowd of men who loaded their phones with the link to home. The connection with Baghdad was constant, the questions always the same: Was it any better? Was it safe to come back? "Stay where you are" was the message from home; there is still too much death here.

CHAPTER FOUR

"NOW IS THE WINTER
OF OUR DISCONTENT"

The Dar al Assad for Culture and Arts is an expression of Syria's ambitions to be the center of Middle East culture. At the entrance, the
signature artwork is a modern colored-glass interpretive sculpture of
the Sword of the Umayyad Caliphs, a reference to a period of Islamic
history when Damascus was the most powerful capital of the Muslim
world. The young president's ambitions for Syria are reflected in the
themes of Western-Arab fusion, demonstrated with classical concerts
by Syria's National Symphony Orchestra and a gleaming blond-wood
paneled lobby as a showcase for Arab painters and sculptors. The Dar
al Assad, or House of Assad, is named for Syria's presidential dynasty.
It was opened in 2004 by President Bashar al-Assad and his wife,
Asma, a British-born Syrian and a former banker at J.P. Morgan. The
ruling couple is also a symbol of Western-Arab fusion: secular, English
speaking, Western-educated Syrians. The president studied ophthal-
mology in London; his sparkling banker-turned-first-lady had a place

at Harvard business school that she gave up to marry into the ruling family.

In 2008, UNESCO designated Damascus the year's "Arab cultural center," and a controversial play, *Richard the III, an Arab Tragedy*, was one event in a year-long festival. The advance publicity was intriguing. An Arab version of Shakespeare's doomed king had been adapted by a young Kuwaiti playwright: "In this world of tribal allegiances, family infighting, and absolute power, the questions of leadership, religion, and foreign intervention at the heart of Shakespeare's play take on powerful new meaning in a modern Arab-Islamic context." The tickets sold out almost at once. The themes of the play tantalizingly echoed the Assad regime's internal dynamics. Family infighting, absolute power, and questions of leadership and religion had all left their mark during the reign of the Assad family. Yet these were forbidden topics in any other public setting. So the well-dressed theater crowd antici- pated a political event as much as a night of drama. Under Syrian law it is illegal for more than five people to gather without a government permit, a measure to restrict organized political opposition to the regime. But this was a theatrical performance and some of Syria's po- litical dissidents gathered among the crowd without concern.

Under the Assads' rule, provocative political theater had been tol- erated since the 1960s—a period during which private companies pre- sented critical dramas designed to engage the intelligentsia of Damascus. The most famous productions came from the "Theater of Thorns," which, known for innovative political satire through song and dance, influenced drama productions throughout the Middle East. The Iraqi exile production of *Selling the Country*, a television satire reflecting on themes of bureaucracy, suppression, and political abuse, was modeled on the innovative political dramas staged earlier in Damascus. Politics in the Middle East is living theater, filled with posturing and inflations of esteem. Theater is the most symbolic and revealing way of observing the intimate details of power. Because it is not intended for the masses, plays are tolerated much more than other media. The audiences are elite, and few.

The audience streamed into the small theater space at the Damascus Opera House, men in baseball caps, some in suits, matrons on cellphones, women in head scarves. As curtain-up approached, and then passed, the audience grew restless. There was more cellphone chatter, interrupted by a minor disturbance at stage right as the surprised audience watched the Assads, the Syrian president and his young wife, take their seats conspicuously in the front row. A few of the theater-goers stood in a reflexive show of respect. There was one persistent clap that quickly died as the stage lights faded to signal the start of the performance.

On stage, Shakespeare's drama of power and betrayal was rendered in a recognizably modern Arab setting. Richard, the Duke of Gloucester, was now the Emir Gloucester, with flowing robes and the mad, menacing charm of the late Iraqi dictator, Saddam Hussein. The scheming Buckingham wore a Western suit and controlled the state-run media and collaborated with the CIA. The themes of the play—modern technology in the service of sophisticated propaganda, religion used to justify atrocities, corruption, and betrayal—were Syrian topics. Everything that was usually *tahta tawila* ("under the table") in Syria was visible, brought to the stage by a sixteenth-century English playwright and adapted for the present-day Middle Eastern context by a thirty-something Kuwaiti artist who was also present in the theater. Watching the drama in the presence of a real-life Arab autocrat provided an additional thrill. The playwright would later compare the experience to Shakespeare and his troupe playing to Queen Elizabeth and her court. The mainly Syrian audience was captivated as much by the drama on stage as by the one in the first row.

Omar Amiralay was thinking of all this when I went to see him a few days after the performance. I had spotted him in the audience, a few rows above mine with the same direct line-of-sight to President

Bashar al-Assad. Amiralay's career as a film documentarian, dissident, and member of Syria's oppressed "civil society" made him a fascinating witness.

"When one of the actors talked about an election where 99.99 percent of the votes are for the leader, so President Assad was laughing. You have seen that?" Indeed, I detected a hearty presidential laugh, even a knee slap, at the absurd tradition in the controlled elections of the Arab world: The reported figure in the actual Syrian referendum in 2000, when Bashar al-Assad had succeeded his father as president, was, in fact, close to 99.99 percent.

"My explanation about this cynical situation," said Amiralay, "when civil society has no force, or represents no danger to the regime, then political criticism becomes an entertainment."

Syrian authorities had jailed many of Syria's most prominent dissidents over the past few years in a crackdown that had decimated "civil society" and put an end to any organized opposition to the government. It was surprising that Amiralay was still willing to talk critically and publicly.

"But there were two hundred people in the audience," I pointed out, noting that the audience members had laughed as heartily as the president.

"It is nothing. It is like a small oil spot," said Amiralay, explaining that the crowd was small and the joke was at the expense of everyone in the audience.

In the practical calculations that count in the region, Bashar al-Assad was a winner. The young president of Syria had been an accidental choice. Years earlier, in a drama worthy of Shakespeare, his uncle, the brother of Hafez al-Assad, had overstepped the boundaries of ambition and had been banished to Paris. Bashar's older brother, Basil, a dashing, forceful character, was the designated successor to Hafez. Bashar had chosen medicine; he expected to be an eye doctor. When the heir apparent, Basil, died in a high-speed car crash in 1994, Bashar was hastily summoned home from London, cutting short his residency at Western Eye Hospital, part of St. Mary's Hospital system in Britain. His father quickly promoted Bashar through the ranks of the military to prepare him for the job ahead. Bashar's only political role before becoming president of Syria was as leader of the Syrian Computer Society. In June 2000, upon the sudden death of Hafez, he became, at the age of thirty-four, the youngest ruler in the Middle East. Eight years on, he had survived a face-off against the global superpower and was still in office when President George W. Bush left his. Standing up to the president of the United States had served Bashar well, and not only in Syrian public opinion. Bashar al-Assad's popularity had consistently risen in the wider Middle East when people were asked:"Which world leader outside your country do you admire most?" For Bashar al-Assad, it was a sign that Syria was regaining its rightful place in the Arab world, an outcome that few in Washington would have predicted.

In the spring of 2003, when Syria's political leaders stood against the U.S. invasion of Iraq, the Syrian"street" rallied behind the regime. Syrians were convinced the invasion was based on American lies about Saddam Hussein's alleged weapons of mass destruction and Saddam's links to Al Qaeda. Syria's leadership challenged President Bush's call to arms and the flaunting of international laws. Syria, ruled by one of the least democratic regimes in the region, was more in-tune with popular sentiment across the Arab world than any other Arab government.

Syrians followed the American invasion of Iraq on television. They watched while smoking hubbly bubbly in the downtown cafés. They gazed up from fierce late-night backgammon games in teahouses. They noted the mayhem on small screens in shops crammed along the cobblestone streets of the Old City, surrounded by the fragrance of cardamom and fresh coffee, and on the flat screens in acrid smoky bars. Syrians examined and analyzed the unfolding chaos in Iraq with anxiety. While they might hate their own ruling regime, they were almost uniformly opposed to an outside power's imposition of regime change in Baghdad, let alone in Damascus.

Unlike most Jordanians, Syrians did not love Saddam Hussein; nor did they see him as the standard-bearer for Sunni Islam against the Shiites of Iran, the view in Saudi Arabia and among other Gulf Arabs. In 1979, Syria was the first Arab country to recognize Iran's new clerical regime, and it supported Tehran during the long Iran-Iraq war of the 1980s. In fact, many Syrians hated Saddam Hussein. During the 1980s, Saddam secretly funded Syria's Muslim Brotherhood in a challenge to the government that brought the country to the brink of civil war. Saddam sent his agents to Syria to arrange car-bomb attacks in the Syrian capital and in the seaside town of Tartous. In return, for decades Syria welcomed Iraq's political exiles, provided a safe haven, and supported plots against Saddam. That is why Iraq's prime minister, Nouri al-Maliki, had ended up in Damascus and spent more than twenty years there in exile.

But while Syrians might have been glad to see the end of Saddam Hussein, the gratification was tempered by anxiety over the U.S. military stationed on Syria's eastern border. "This was an emotional time," explained a Western diplomat posted in Damascus. "Assad's response was driven by the street," he said. Sunni Arab rulers in Egypt, Saudi Arabia, and Jordan had quietly acquiesced as President George W. Bush ignored their warnings and prepared for war. Syria's traditional anti-American stand was reinforced by the overwhelming clamor of its citizens.

"The advisors around the young and untested new president, Bashar, predicted that the American invasion would end in tears. They didn't want to be on the losing side. His father had always picked the winners," the diplomat said.

In 1991, Hafez al-Assad had backed President George H. W. Bush against Saddam Hussein in the first Gulf war. In the run-up to the conflict, the Syrian military participated in joint training exercises in the Saudi desert with American trainers who schooled Syrian tank drivers in close air support (CAS). This was a tactic that required extreme coordination between American air power and the Arab armies on the ground. It represented the closest-ever relationship between the Syrian military and that of the United States. Syrians were eventually convinced that this was a worthy Arab cause. The defense of Kuwait was portrayed as an Arab nation illegally invaded by a reckless Saddam Hussein. At the time, Hafez al-Assad benefited from his decision to support the United States. After Saddam's army was routed, the Gulf Arabs showered Syria with investments; the Bush administration effectively allowed Damascus to extend its control over neighboring Lebanon, where Syria's army settled in for an extended stay. The warmed relationship with Washington led to Syria's participation in the 1991 Madrid peace process and almost a decade of U.S.-brokered negotiations between Israel and Syria.

The 2003 war in Iraq was the inheritance for the sons of presidential fathers, Bashar al-Assad and George W. Bush. But this time the stakes were totally different. In the first Gulf war, President George H. W. Bush had stopped short of ousting Saddam, a conclusion his son did not intend to repeat. This time, Bashar al-Assad's survival, along with the survival of his regime, depended on a keen analysis of the consequences of the collapse of a neighboring Arab state. The forcible overthrow of a secular Arab regime that did not submit to U.S. policy goals was not a precedent that Bashar al-Assad could afford to support.

Once the war started, Syria's top Muslim religious authority, Sheik Ahmad Kaftaro, encouraged fighters to go to Iraq. "I call on Muslims everywhere to use all means possible to thwart the aggression, including martyr operations against the belligerent American, British, and Zionist invaders," he said. His call to arms was faxed to international news agencies. Kaftaro, though a popular religious figure, could not have issued such a politically charged religious edict without complicit support from the regime.

At the central bus station, young Syrians and other Arab men lined up to use the public pay phone to dial long-distance for final goodbyes. They had come to Damascus to get a place on one of the many buses provided by the Iraqi interest section or used their last cash reserves to buy a seat on one of the long-haul Syrian taxis for the journey east.

While Syrian officials denied facilitating the travel of volunteer fighters across the border, the exodus was a public event. Another diplomat posted in Damascus at the time told me that when he got a call from an American intelligence analyst in Washington asking if he could confirm that volunteer fighters were moving from the Syrian capital, he answered, "Dude, I can see them outside my window!" In an irony of placement in the Syrian capital, the U.S. and Iraqi embassies were neighbors. The transport buses were parked on a shared street.

Bashar had widespread popular support for his hard-line stand against the Americans' war in Iraq. In time, however, Syrians became alarmed by the rapid collapse of Saddam's regime in Baghdad and the chaos that followed. Would the Americans flex their muscles again? Syrians spoke aloud of fears that the Americans had plans to march to their city, too. They heard the voices of influential Americans calling for the invasion of Syria. For the first time ever, in the spring of 2003, there were air-raid drills in Damascus. American soldiers were on Syria's doorstep. Regime change was momentarily a viable tool in the American strategy for the Middle East.

"It was ad hoc, people were clamoring to help the Iraqi resistance," the diplomat told me. The rush to Iraq was unstoppable because the American invasion had upset the traditional sectarian power arrangements in the Middle East. Sunni Arab tribes on Syria's border had bloodlines—first cousins, uncles, families, marriages—that extended into Iraq. Did Syria encourage the professional jihadists who bought one-way tickets and landed at the Damascus airport or drove over the border from Lebanon and Jordan? That seems unlikely considering secular Syria's antipathy toward religiously inspired militants within Syria's borders. But they were allowed to depart unhindered. Syria, ruled mostly by minority Alawites, was adding a "Sunni Card" to strengthen a weak hand against the American project in Iraq. "Syrian officials saw themselves helping the effort. It wasn't clear when the 'professionals' started coming. The Syrians were always ambivalent about these people. I don't think the Syrians wanted a flood, it was enough to cause a nuisance," the diplomat said, referring to the Al Qaeda–inspired recruits who joined the enthusiastic amateurs. But there was a flood, nonetheless. Professional jihadists eventually gathered in Syria, joined an underground system that grew to accommodate them, and arranged for their trip on the smugglers' trails over the border into Iraq. Martyrdom in Iraq for homegrown radicals and transiting Arab fighters was the preferred and pragmatic outcome.

This was more than a "nuisance" for Washington. The extensive jihadist network fed and fueled the insurgency in Iraq and the sectarian civil war that followed. The Bush administration demanded that Syria halt the traffic by enforcing security along the long border with Iraq. To step up the pressure, Washington actively worked to enforce Syria's diplomatic isolation in Europe and the Middle East and put in place new sanctions against the Syrian government and individuals within the leadership. Vice President Dick Cheney's formulation summed up the approach: The administration did not reward bad behavior.

Washington decided to overlook the cooperation in 1991 and see a longer trend of Syrian bad behavior. Syria was a charter member of the State Department's designated "states that sponsor terrorism," listed since 1979. In the lead-up to the war, the Bush administration warned Syria about the more recent lucrative relationship with Saddam Hussein. An oil-smuggling scheme through the Kirkuk-Banyas pipeline had undermined United Nations sanctions put in place against Iraq in August 1990. After the invasion, the seemingly easy transit of Islamist militants heading east to join Iraq's resistance army further outraged the Pentagon. The foreign force, though a small percentage of the combatants in Iraq, transformed the battlefield for an American army unprepared and untrained in counterinsurgency.

President Bush had not specifically named Syria as part of the "axis of evil," but his administration considered Bashar al-Assad to be an obstacle to ambitious plans for the democratic transformation of the region. Bush accused Bashar of supporting Iraq's insurgency, backing the murder of a former Lebanese prime minister that undermined Lebanon's fragile democracy, and encouraging terrorism against Israel by arming Hezbollah and allowing militant Palestinian leaders to operate openly in Damascus.

Recalling those days in Damascus, in the run-up to the momentous U.S. invasion of Iraq, the Western diplomat, still serving in the region, reflected on Syria's policy choices. He pointed out that ideologically and by inclination, and given geography and the regime's obsession with self-preservation, Bashar al-Assad had no choice but to stand against the war, stepping over the stark line laid out by the Bush administration. "You are either with us or against us, that was what the Americans said," he quoted. The administration had adopted a Manichean approach that eliminated the nuance, the subtle give-and-take essential to American diplomacy, particularly in the Middle East: "Common sense went out the window." Even now, the diplomat in-

sisted his frank views had to be delivered without name or country attached. He had warned his own government that turning Syria into
an enemy would be a mistake. Washington had done just that and
paid a price in Iraq and in the region.

Damascus faced instability on its borders and the undeniable presence of surviving Islamist militants who used Syria as a path to Iraq
and returned as hardened veterans ready to threaten what they considered an apostate regime. By 2005, Syria's multiple intelligence agencies had begun a massive crackdown on militants and anyone else
considered a threat to internal security. The cost of the war to Syria
"hasn't been that high," the diplomat judged. Considering that regime
survival was the ultimate goal, the strategy was worth the price.

In the early days of the war, the border was wide open for the first
time in decades. Smugglers restored the desert routes ferrying sheep,
cigarettes, and fuel to an expanding Iraqi market. The militants joined
the underground highway, hauling weapons and the bundles of cash
that comprised the operating budget of Al Qaeda in Mesopotamia.
Under pressure from Iraq and America, the Syrians eventually con-
structed a three-foot-high sand berm along the border, increased the
border posts to more than five hundred, and stationed additional border guards. But berms and borders divide nations, not tribes. In the
Middle East, tribal loyalty is more important than national citizenship.
The historical connections between the tribes on both sides of the
border were revived by the American invasion of Iraq. Greater Syria,
long extinct, flexed its remembered cultural muscles.

The Syrians were able to squeeze off the jihadist traffic but not
entirely stop it. There were too many moving parts to control. The
border-post guards were rarely rotated and became easy to bribe; some
tribal families sympathized with Al Qaeda's agenda in Iraq and facilitated the crossing. The bearded foreigners who arrived in darkness
and stayed a few days or a few weeks were quiet men who did nothing

to disturb the peace in the villages of Syrian farmers and peasants on the border.

Syrians say they repeatedly asked the Americans and the Iraqis to form a joint security command to stop the problems, but the answer was always the same. U.S. officials tied cooperation with larger political goals. There was a long list: Comply with a United Nations request over the investigation into the assassination of former Lebanese Prime Minister Rafiq Hariri; stop support for Hamas and Hezbollah; stop meddling in Lebanon. In October 2008, the Bush administration approved a raid across the Syrian border, killing eight people, one of whom was said to be a senior Al Qaeda operative who had operated freely on Syria's border.

On the other side of the border, the Americans were stretched too thin to patrol the more than three hundred miles of possible crossings. And the Iraqi border guards who began to take on the job were poorly equipped, often running out of fuel and the will to do the job. They took bribes to look the other way. The border remained as porous as on the Syrian side.

During the early months of the Bush administration, the cautious approach of Bashar al-Assad had brought renewed hopes for more positive relations between Washington and Damascus—at least in the traditional diplomatic camp headquartered at Colin Powell's State Department. The Bush White House remained wary of the change in Damascus. The attitude, explained Aaron David Miller, who had served six secretaries of state, was: "There was a virus and we don't want to get too close. They are not on the right side of our philosophical and ideological view of the world. Assad Jr. was always going to be an extremely difficult problem to resolve."

In the first year of Bashar al-Assad's rule, the terrorist attacks of September 11, 2001, came as both a tragedy and an opportunity. Syria saw the Bush administration's "global war on terror" as an opening to broader relations with Washington. Syria had fought the Muslim Brotherhood in the early 1980s and was hostile to militant Islam. This was one conflict where the Bush administration and Damascus were on the same side. Bashar denounced the September 11 attacks and in a radio address called for "international cooperation to eradicate all forms of terrorism." Like his father, Bashar did not deny support for Hezbollah, Hamas, and Islamic Jihad (groups he considered to be resistance movements), but he offered cooperation against Al Qaeda, which was a threat to his secular regime. Syria approved unprecedented access to the FBI and the CIA for intelligence operations inside Syria. There was a rich vein of intelligence in the northern Syrian city of Aleppo, where Mohammed Atta, one of the nineteen hijackers, had lived in the 1990s while working on a dissertation about urban planning. Syria shared intelligence gained from interrogations of Muhammad Haydar Zammar, the man suspected of recruiting Mohammed Atta to carry out the 9/11 attacks. State Department officials repeatedly declared that Syrian cooperation "had saved American lives." In particular, Syrian intelligence had warned the CIA of an impending Al Qaeda attack against the fifth fleet headquartered in Bahrain, which, if successful, would have killed a large number of Americans.

But for the Bush White House, it wasn't enough that Syria should cooperate in the war on terrorism, something that, administration officials pointed out, was in Syria's own national interest. President Bush considered authoritarian regimes *per se* the root cause of terrorism. He raised the bar for Syria and other authoritarian regimes in the Middle East: Good relations with the United States, he said, "will require the decent treatment of their own people." Global freedom was an American ideal, but Bush said it was also "the urgent requirement of our national security and the calling of our time." Powerful voices in Washington, among the neo-conservative camp and supporters of

Israel, regarded Bashar's regime and the instruments of oppression in Syria as part of the problem.

In December 2003, with Saddam easily toppled, President Bush imposed new economic sanctions on Damascus. A year later, Bush joined forces with French President Jacques Chirac to support a United Nations resolution demanding that Syria end its military occupation of Lebanon, which had begun during the 1976 civil war. In February 2005, Washington recalled its ambassador from Damascus after a powerful bomb in Beirut killed Rafiq Hariri—as noted, the former billionaire prime minister of Lebanon, and also a critic of the Syrian regime. A United Nations investigation promptly linked Syria to the Hariri murder. Each step was designed to pile on the pressure, to deepen Syria's isolation, to undermine Damascus. When Bashar was asked, What did he think the U.S. administration wanted from him, he answered, "I don't know. This is the problem."

In Damascus, Bashar al-Assad's picture was already unavoidable at bus stops, behind cash registers, and on the back windows of passenger cars, but as Washington intensified its pressure on Damascus, his singular image also began to appear on street corners, traffic islands, and fluttering banners hanging from lamp posts. In the early days of his presidency, Syrians made jokes about the pictures. "The Father, the Son, and the Holy Ghost" is what they called the trinity of Hafez, the late president, depicted with his two sons, Basil and Bashar. But from 2006, more often Bashar was depicted alone in heroic poses, staring into the future, his features softened to a Hollywood-movie-poster handsome. The largest photograph, two stories high, was installed outside the ancient Hamadiya market and showed a smiling Bashar waving over the slogan "I believe in Syria."

After the Iraq project stalled for President Bush, European ambassadors and foreign ministers started coming back to Damascus for consultations. American senators, both Democrats and Republicans, broke Syria's isolation with highly publicized visits aimed at showing concern for Iraqi refugees, or to gain insights into negotiations with Israel, or Lebanon. Demands that Syria adopt America's favored model—majority rule balanced by minority rights and the rule of law—were dropped in the face of a more realistic assessment that there was no alternative on the horizon for governing Syria. Like Iraq before the war, Syria had no nongovernmental institutions that could maintain national unity or channel political expression. There was still only the Baath party and the security apparatus. And Bashar al-Assad.

The dapper Assad—a man who always dressed in an expensive, fashionably cut business suit and had his hair close-cropped and his mustache trimmed in European and not Islamic fashion—nonetheless quietly tied his fortunes to the revolutionary theocracy in Iran, even more closely than had his father. In a regime that prized secularism, Bashar was a frequent guest at the mosques of Damascus. He welcomed a long list of official Iranian visitors who arrived in flowing robes and turbans. He consulted with Tehran on regional politics in Iraq and Lebanon. He bet that the regional power that would be left standing when the dust of war settled would be not America but Iran. But Syrian policy has always been guided by expediency, an outlook passed down from his father. Behind the scenes, in late 2006, Bashar had sent some of his most trusted insiders to explore secret negotiations with Israel as well. Bashar, after all, was his father's son.

The Turkish prime minister, Recep Tayip Erdogan, acted as the broker. The indirect negotiations commenced at an official level with Israel's foreign ministry team and Syrian negotiators in separate hotels. As the negotiations progressed, the Israeli and Syrian delegates were housed in the same hotel and Prime Minister Erdogan shuttled between rooms. Over time, the negotiating teams hammered out a detailed blueprint for the return of the Golan Heights, the volcanic plateau overlooking northern Galilee captured by Israel in the 1967 war. For Syria, the alliance with Iran was on the table, as was Syria's support for anti-Israeli groups such as Hezbollah and Iran.

The bargaining was a sign that Syria had returned to its historic roots. Trade has always been the center of Syrian culture with its ancient souks and merchant elites. A deal with Israel to return the Golan Heights could have momentous implications for the rest of the region. The bargaining reached its highest level in the fall of 2008. Ehud Olmert, Israel's prime minister, arrived in Istanbul to review a list of security questions about the Golan that Israeli negotiators had posed to the Syrian team. These were the last details to iron out— trust-building measures as much as negotiation points. Syria had answered the questions as a sign of serious intent. Erdogan again served as the go-between: he was on the phone with the Syrian president and face-to-face with the Israeli prime minister. Olmert signaled his approval to continue the talks. Syria's response to the security questions had been reviewed by the highest level of the Israeli government and was thought satisfactory. The differences were now so narrow that a historic breakthrough seemed in sight. The timing was right. In a few weeks' time, the new American president-elect, Barack Obama, would take office. Obama had signaled his endorsement of direct Syria-Israel talks with American involvement, a stark departure from the Bush administration's approach. Top Obama officials had reached out to the Syrian ambassador in Washington to demonstrate that the new rules for the Middle East would include traditional diplomacy. Olmert said he would need a bit more time, one more round of talks in Tel Aviv, but the perception in Damascus and in Ankara was that the stage was set—to use a singularly appropriate metaphor. Recalling what would become the last negotiating round, the Turkish prime minister said in an interview later: "On that night, we were very close to reaching an agreement between the two parties. It was agreed they were going to talk until the end of the week to come to a [positive] outcome. Olmert's last sentence [as he left] was, 'As soon as I get back I will consult with my colleagues and get back to you.'" Recep Taypip Edogan and Bashar al-Assad waited. Four days later, on December 27, Israeli airstrikes in Gaza, and the devastating ground campaign that followed, postponed indefinitely the prospects for the final negotiations. Soon Olmert was out of power, replaced by a hard-line government with no commitment to bargain away territory.

But Bashar al-Assad was not the Saddam-like Richard III in play at the Damascus Opera House. He was not a paranoid tyrant whose kingdom lay in ruins because of American intervention. Bashar was a pragmatist in regional politics. The talks with Israel had broken down, but not permanently. In the view of much of the world, the fault was in Israel, not in Syria. Negotiations could resume when conditions were ripe for an American president looking for an avenue for change in the region with a margin for success. This was the lesson of politics manifest in the Arabic production of *Richard the III, an Arab Tragedy*. The play was a reflection on the fragility of power, and Bashar al-Assad understood that aspect well. He had steered a cunning survival course and was achieving diplomatic and political gains. Assad stood with the audience at the conclusion of the drama staged in the Opera House. He energetically applauded the production and walked calmly through the theater lobby among the throngs of Syrians who appreciated the ancient tale of power politics gone badly wrong and their young president who so far got it right.

CHAPTER FIVE

IDENTITY AND
REPRESSION

Syria and Iraq, Damascus and Baghdad, long the rival capitals in Islamic history, and geopolitical rivals in modern times, are consumed with the question of identity. In one, a Baathist state had tightened its grip on power; in the other, it had been blown away, opening a vacuum into which the politics of rival identities had flowed with catastrophic results. For Iraq, the forces that divided the country after 2003 were far stronger than the history that had unified the people. Banditry and breakdown in Iraq had led to mass exodus and internal displacement. In 2009, the unanswered question "What is Iraq?" discomforted Arab neighbors and kept the exiles from returning. They were still unwilling to bet their lives and the future on their homeland until they were sure of the answer.

The new Iraqi constitution, approved in a national referendum in October 2005, was designed to define a new identity for Iraq. Instead it only raised more questions. For the first time Islam was declared the official religion of Iraq. The second article contained the clause "no law may be enacted that contradicts the established provisions of Islam," which was at the expense of Iraq's non-Muslim minorities and considered a step backward for women's rights according to secular Iraqis. The constitutional framers included a phrase that defined Iraq as part of the Islamic world, its citizens part of the Arab nation, which was an affront to the non-Arab Kurds. In northern Iraq, many Kurds considered Baghdad a foreign capital. For more than a decade, Arabic was scarcely spoken on the streets of Sulemaniyah and Irbil, the cosmopolitan Kurdish cities in the mountains. The new constitution supported the idea of federalism, which the Kurds embraced to protect their hard-won autonomy, but in practice might mean an Iraq of three sectarian-defined parts with a weak central government and no unifying identity at all.

Islamist jihadists espousing Al Qaeda's views determined that "non-believers" had no place in Iraq and targeted Christians for conversion or death. These merciless men hated all things Shia as well. In their literal-minded totalitarian worldview, Shiite rituals were imported from Persia and constituted proof of idolatry. In their heterodox interpretation of Islam, Shiites were "rejectors" and not Muslims at all. The equally bigoted secular Sunni insurgents referred to Shiites in the Baghdad government as "Safavids," an aspersion that implied Persian origins with no right to Iraqi identity.

The hatred was returned. Many Shiites were convinced those who joined Saddam's Baath party had forfeited a role in the liberated country. Radical Shiite assassination squads targeted top Sunni Baathists, forcing many more to flee. Within the government, a campaign of debaathification disproportionately punished Sunnis by denying them jobs and canceling their pensions. At the same time, Iraq's Shiite leaders insisted that they were Arab Shiites, not Persian, who shared a long history with all of Iraq's Arabs, Sunnis and Christians alike. For the first time in history, Iraq's future was in Arab Shiite hands, but

Iraq's new rulers were unsure of how to use power after centuries of disinheritance and persecution, and uncertain of the country's political destination.

For the exiles, the outcome of the struggle to define Iraqi identity was vital to the prospects for their return; they simply had to know the essential nature of the new nation-state of Iraq. Historically, Iraq was the frontier country between Arabia and Persia—in Ottoman times, tolerant of the broad diversity of sects and tribes that had settled in the harsh deserts, marshlands, and fertile plains of the land of two rivers. In modern history, Iraq was a counterweight to Iran's regional power. From the 1920s, Iraq forcefully imposed a strident Arabism on the diverse population, and then from 1979 until Saddam's demise was a bulwark against Shiite Iran's 1979 Islamic Revolution. The American invasion had deposed a Sunni Pan-Arab regime and overturned the established order in the region.

"Arabs didn't choose the mix, it was the retreating colonial powers," explained Rami Khoury, a Palestinian Christian scholar and longtime colleague of mine, when I raised questions of identity in his office at the American University in Beirut. In the Middle East, conversations about identity often start with a reference to colonial borders drawn in the self-interest of British and French imperialists in the early twentieth century that created nation-states by dividing groups and tribes.

"Iraq is typical of this pattern. Then [in 2003], a foreign invasion wiped away the state, so the people had to reconfigure and renegotiate the power relationship," Khoury explained. "And when you are dealing with billions of dollars in oil revenues, and the resentments of previous rule of the Baathists, and the deliberate provocation by Al Qaeda, the combination of all these things, plus the sectarian cleansing, these are issues [of identity] that have to be sorted out."

Saddam had exaggerated sectarian cleavages to prevent any unified opposition against him and then held the tension in check through a powerful state security apparatus and authoritarian rule. When the state collapsed, Iraqis took refuge in tribal and religious loyalties, often not out of conviction but because they believed they had to belong somewhere. A country that was forced together by the army was now torn apart by the mosques. While the exiles had fled for safety, many had also run from a raw sectarian identification that had swept the country and replaced the older nationalist identity of the educated class of Baghdad.

"These are countries that have never defined themselves. They've never agreed on 'who are we—what are our core value systems.' Is it Islam—Arab nationalism? This hasn't happened in any Arab country— we have not seen any country go through a process where its own people in a normal situation can define it themselves," said Khoury. For Iraq, the more immediate question was: How are citizens going to live together within the borders?

Arab states had managed before under the dual constraints of the Cold War and unabashedly autocratic governments, indulged by the West and Soviet Union alike. In Khoury's view, the abnormal condition in the region, which explained much of the turbulence, is a simple fact: The region is still run by autocrats. "These are still societies in a pre-state condition," according to Khoury. The nation-states, created to serve imperialist colonial designs, handed over to local potentates, flush with oil revenues and indulged by a superpower conflict, were not prepared to manage themselves as stable, modern political entities. Nothing in their history had prepared them for such a role. Not then and not now.

While far from a "normal situation," for the first time in its history Iraq was struggling to define a post-war identity within a democratic framework—with competing points of view—a messy, dysfunctional process that was monitored from Arab capitals with reactions that ranged from unease to alarm.

"The real unforgiveable sin in the eyes of the neighbors is G.W.S., 'Governing while Shia,'" explained Ryan Crocker, the U.S. ambassador to Baghdad from 2007 to 2009, which were some of the most turbulent years for Iraq.

"It's true—sad, but there it is—the prejudice runs deep," said Crocker. Since his retirement from the State Department, he was more forthcoming with his observations of a region he knew as well as anyone in the U.S. government. An Arabic speaker, Crocker had been posted in the Middle East for more than two decades. In 2002, at the request of Secretary of State Colin Powell, he had worked on a secret memo on Iraq, a dozen single-spaced pages titled "The Perfect Storm." The memo was a brutally frank prediction of the fragmentation and chaos that would follow the U.S. invasion, in which Crocker warned that the majority Shiites, along with the Kurds, would likely vie for dominance over the minority Sunnis. He also cautioned that Iraq's neighbors, including Iran, Syria, and Saudi Arabia, would try to influence a weakened Iraqi state. Ambassador Crocker saw all of his predictions come to pass from the U.S. embassy in Baghdad, as a fragile Iraq struggled to define itself anew. The regional powers watched with intense interest. Was this because one piece of the regional Sunni power structure had been displaced, or because Iraq was defining itself? "I think that is exactly what is going on," said Crocker of the latter choice. "Their neighbors have tried and are trying to influence Iraq, but Iraq, being Iraq, is pretty resistant to that kind of thing. The Saudis look at their eastern province [with a large Shiite population], and say, 'Oh, man, a Shia-led state [in Iraq] where it's all out in the open, it's public, and it's democracy. That is not good for the Arabs.'"

The 1920 state system had defined the colonial borders in the Arab world without regard to a fair share of power or the distribution of resources to the majority and minority groups within those borders. Mindful of this history, in 2005, the newly empowered Shiite majority in Iraq backed the constitutionally guaranteed federalism within Iraq's borders to address the distribution of power and resources away from Baghdad where, under Saddam, the Sunnis had reaped the overwhelming benefits of the centralized state. Shiite politicians talked about a super region of nine provinces from Basra in the south through the Shiite shrine cities of Karbala and Najaf to the outskirts of the capital. Others referred to this new region as "Shiitestan," in much the same way as the Kurds referred to their autonomous region in the north as Kurdistan. "Sunnistan" would be an oil-less rump in the north and west of Baghdad.

"This opens up a huge problem for many people in the Arab world who fear decentralization," said Rami Khoury, "where you get people in other countries who say—I want my autonomous region, too. The Shiites of eastern Saudi Arabia are one example." There were groups in every country in the Middle East who could make a case for autonomy, or even independence, and some of them—in areas ranging from the Gulf States to Egypt—had been emboldened by the changes in Iraq.

While Baghdad's search for identity had resulted in rampant sectarianism and violence, Damascus was undergoing something of a quiet revival. The two capitals had long been rivals since the early days of Islamic history. In the seventh century, Damascus was the capital of the Muslim world, the seat of the first caliphate and the vast Uyymyad empire. Then in 750, the caliphate moved east to Baghdad and incorporated a conquered Persia as part of the victorious Abbasid dynasty. The Damascus-Baghdad rivalry was revived in the twentieth century with the establishment of rival Baath parties.

When I first came to Damascus in the 1980s, Hafez al-Assad was president, the Soviet Union was Syria's Cold War patron, and the city was a drab rundown place, an Arab imitation of an East European capital. Damascus is a boom town now. Flocks of construction cranes hover over the city. Wealthy Syrians turn dilapidated traditional houses in the Old City into historically correct boutique hotels. Almost every week another brand-name coffee shop opens. Lattes seem to be the official drink of a new class of well-dressed young Syrian customers. Syrians could now put money in private banks and use credit cards. In 2009, a stock market opened (although only seven companies' stocks were traded on the first day). Private universities were flourishing. In the American plan, Baghdad was supposed to be the next capital of free-market capitalism. However, Bashar al-Assad had been the one to crack open the strictest socialist economy in the Middle East—he said he was following the Chinese model, at a pace he believed Syria could manage, which fell some way short of offering total freedom of expression, but goods and modernity were flooding in. Internet cafés existed in most Damascus neighborhoods, usually packed with young Syrians surfing past midnight. Everyone had a cellphone. Syrian culture had more in common with the West—the United States and Europe—than with its closest ally Tehran and the emerging state of Iraq.

One of the most popular radio stations in the city, Madina FM, featured a show called *Good Morning Syria*, the highest-rated program in Damascus. The radio host, with the improbable name of Honey Sayed, chatted with call-in listeners in Arabic and English, and led radio discussions on controversial social subjects such as child abuse and homosexuality. Syrians watched *Oprah* on satellite television and voted by cellphone in pop-song competitions run by Lebanese TV. American rap music flooded the airwaves; 50 Cent was a particular favorite. Syrians were defining themselves as consumers, but in Syria, too, a national identity was still under debate. A public conversation was considered dangerous and deemed illegal, in a list of vague provisions prohibiting the publication of "inaccurate information" or "harming national unity." Still, the authoritarianism of Bashar's regime afforded some protections for Syria's diverse ethnicities and religions.

But Damascus, for all its unique antiquity, felt fragile—as if modern Damascus could not control the forces that had kept the region on the boil since the American army marched into Baghdad.

Secular Baathist ideology has kept religious and sectarian tensions in check, enforced by multiple security services. But it's a precarious strategy—as the sudden demise of Baathist autocracy in Iraq proved only too vividly. On the surface, at least, Syria had shifted national identity toward a grander vision of "Arabism" and the claim to be its "beating heart." Among the older generation there was an illusion of greatness, demonstrated in the lingering idea of "Greater Syria," a borderless realm that included Lebanon, Jordan, and Israel, plus the Gaza strip. The romance of pan-Arabism still burned as an identity that encompassed a region larger than the borders imposed by colonial powers.

Many of the country's ruling elite, including President Bashar al-Assad, are members of the Alawite sect, an offshoot of Shiite Islam. Alawites were oppressed for centuries (and considered to be heretics by Muslim extremists). Alawites, as well as other minorities, prospered in Syria's secular Baathist system, often through the military. The rise of Bashar's father, Hafez al-Assad, is a typical Alawite story. He was the first in his family to attend high school, but the bright student from an oppressed minority had no money for college. He gained an advanced education through the Syrian Military Academy and completed further technical studies in the Soviet Union. Assad launched a coup d'état from his post as defense secretary and thereafter consolidated the power of the central state. Secular Syria has been surprisingly stable over the forty years of Assad rule, even though the ruling elite are from a minority Shiite sect governing a majority Sunni population.

But at the beginning of the twenty-first century Baathism was a spent revolutionary force and Syria was being hammered by more dynamic movements. The Islamists presented one challenge by disregarding all colonial borders and dreaming of a restored caliphate ruled under an angry, pitiless brand of Sunni Islam that would sweep away Alawites and all the other minorities in the Middle East. The American project in Iraq brought counter-demands from Washington. This alternate challenge, echoed by Arab reformers, called for a Middle East of defined borders and democracy. A stronger challenge came with Iraq's sectarian war, which stirred a strong sense of sectarian identity all over the region. With Iraqi families arriving by the thousands every day, Syrians worried that what had happened in full view across their Eastern border was about to tear apart Syrian identity as well.

Syrians were horrified by the accounts of sectarian bloodletting and security breakdowns that they heard firsthand from Iraqi families piling into low-rent neighborhoods surrounding the capital. An older generation had been taught to believe that Lebanon's democracy led to civil war there. Now, this already suspicious population evaluated Baghdad's tragedy as the inevitable consequence of the importation of American-style democracy. In the historic commercial capital, Damascenes prized stability and security—and they supported leaders who provided both. The ancient streets and alleyways of the Old City were surrounded by thick walls and seven gates to protect against invaders. But Syrians were beginning to realize that the walls, even the borders, couldn't stop the spillover from Iraq.

"If democracy brings such chaos in the region, and especially the destruction of society, as it did in Iraq, it's absolutely normal, and I think it's absolutely a wise position from the people to be afraid to imagine how it would be in Syria," Omar Amiralay explained, in evaluating the toll of American policies on the reform movement in Syria. "I think that people at the end said, 'Well, it is better to keep this government. We know them, and we don't want to go to this civil war, and to live this apocalyptic image of change, with civil war and sectarianism and blood."'

Omar Amiralay, an elegant man with swept-back graying hair, delivered his sentences slowly and precisely in French-accented English. He had arranged our meeting at an art gallery in an upscale neighborhood in Damascus. The front garden, on a leafy street, was a respite from the choking traffic. Amiralay weighed his criticisms carefully, a skill honed over a long career as a political activist. Syrian jails were filled with dissidents who had gotten the equation wrong. Almost every time I returned to Syria there were reports of another late-night arrest. Critical speech, in public or in print, required a temperature reading in a country where the powers inside Syria's intelligence agencies put on foul-weather gear before Syria's small band of dissidents ever felt the rain. Syria operated not under the consistent application of a rule of law but, rather, under the rule of uncertainty. It was a refined and effective tool of control through fear. Even the most experienced dissidents periodically stepped over lines they hadn't seen and landed in jail. Syria's emergency laws, in place since 1963, gave the regime the power to arrest anyone without stating a cause.

Amiralay's lament for the defeat of Syria's opposition—a consequence, he believed, of the war in Iraq—was a matter of degree. There had been no organized opposition to the government, no recognized dissident leader with broad grassroots support, no real rival to the controlling Baath party. Rather, Syria's opposition was a collection of intellectual critics from a broad mix of political outlooks: Baathist reformers, Islamists, Marxists, and human rights activists. Most of them were as anti-American as the government. Their organizing principle was a scathing critique of the corrupt practices of the ruling elite and some disparate ideas on how to define a different future. But that was it. In the first few years of Bashar al-Assad's rule, his authoritarian regime tolerated a level of political expression even as the regime largely ignored it.

In the 1980s, during Hafez al-Assad's rule, conversations with the political opposition were difficult and dangerous to arrange. By 2005, it was stunningly easy. The dissidents were eager to meet me and confidently outlined corruption at the highest levels of government. They named names with documents and testimonials to back up the allegations. They discussed grand plans to change the system. I spent long evenings listening to political gatherings small enough to be held in living rooms. I was invited for meals with dissident families and I interviewed activists, even visiting them in offices openly monitored by the police. Most of these critics had been seasoned by months, sometimes years in jail, often in solitary confinement. Among them were second- and third-generation dissidents who had dared stand up against Hafez al-Assad, yet hoped that his son would be more amenable to pluralism in Syria.

When the new president opened the country to the Internet, satellite television, and cellphones, opposition figures used the new communication tools to speak out in English and Arabic. However, as Amiralay pointed out, the opposition posed no real challenge to the regime. Dissidence, ignored by Washington, was finally silenced in Syria after Washington's venture in Iraq convinced more timid citizens that radical ideas and sudden upheavals were too big a risk. The regime had a freer hand to crack down accordingly.

Acknowledging sectarianism remained a taboo in Syria. The Alawite president set a model for assimilation when he married a Sunni, but intermarriage in Syria was rare. The strains in Syria's national identity often came out in casual conversations. A Sunni human rights lawyer told me in an angry whisper that he was convinced Iranians were converting Sunnis to Shiites across the country. He had no evidence supporting his outrage over what he imagined were mass conversions, but he was sure Iranian clerics were bribing poor Syrian villagers to adopt Shiite practices. An Italian landlord told me a story about a Christian contractor who had renovated the bathrooms in her traditional Syrian house. He had agreed to her specifications that the toilets would not be in keeping with the Muslim practice of facing away from Mecca while one was sitting on the commode. He had glee-fully taken the job, she told me, so he could "fuck the Muslims."

Omar Amiralay's opposition was purely secular. He had adopted Marxism as a student in Paris, and when he came home to make his first documentary in 1970, he was intrigued by the government's am-bitious development projects for the poorest region of the country. This film, *Attempt at the Euphrates Dam,* was a glorification of the Asad Dam, the largest water-engineering project in the country. But he soon discovered that the project was plagued by corruption and disruptions. His later documentaries probed the underpinnings of the regime, the Baath party in particular—an ideology he believed had stunted development and a national identity for his country. One such film followed up on his earlier work documenting the dam on the Eu-phrates; but Amiralay's own views had hardened, as evidenced by his controversial working title: "Fifteen Reasons Why I Hate the Baath Party." Even with the more innocuous final title, *A Flood in Baath Country,* the documentary was banned in Syria, though readily avail-able there on DVD.

Like many Syrians, Amiralay had believed in the "Damascus Spring" of 2000, and he had signed a manifesto for a Syrian democratic oppo-sition movement. It was an optimistic time, the year that Bashar al-Assad came to power. One of Bashar's first orders was to instruct Syria's state-run media to use "balanced and logical information and avoid magnification, exaggeration and glorification." In another instruction, he banned the media from using the terms *immortal president* and *for-ever* when referring to his presidential term. It seemed that Syria was turning a page, but the first round of arrests began within a year.

However, this was a different kind of repression, explained Ami-ralay: more delicate, different from the brutal tactics of the past. "They found an intelligent way to proceed with qualitative repression rather than quantitative. In the past, they would put hundreds and thousands of people in prison."

In 1982, Bashar's father had put down a rebellion of the Muslim Brotherhood, sending in Syrian troops to quell an uprising in the city of Hama. In a two-week artillery bombardment that leveled parts of the city, the fundamentalists were crushed and thousands of civilians were killed or imprisoned. The confrontation brought the country to the edge of civil war. Even today, it remains a capital offense in Syria to belong to the outlawed Muslim Brotherhood.

But since then the government had successfully "trained the civil society," according to Amiralay. "That is why, after 2000 and the arrival of Bashar to power, the regime discovered they can arrest just ten people, or one prominent figure within the intelligentsia, and they can gain a period of calm. And I think that they win with this politics of repression."

Syria was a confusing place. On the one hand, we could sit openly for hours talking about politics on a pleasant afternoon in the dappled shade. Amiralay could diagnose the failures of regime policy to an American journalist without fear of arrest at that moment or later in the evening. Syria had never been as repressive as the old Iraq and now, under Bashar, there were visible improvements that Amiralay could not deny. Even the most ardent dissidents cautioned that Syria needed gradual change to maintain stability. The dispute with Bashar's regime, it seemed, was over the timeline.

"Maybe I am a special case. But they have never arrested somebody for a cultural or an artistic act," Amiralay offered, anticipating my question because many of Syria's most prominent activists had been jailed. The risk came to dissidents, he explained, "only when they talk politics. Not when they write a book or they write a poem. They don't have this habit of arresting artists."

Repressive regimes have an understandable logic for allowing some criticisms and banning others. Permitting critiques that come in the form of films, plays, or novels can even serve the regime's purposes. In a poor country like Syria, the audience for art is limited and the members of the intellectual elite who produce that art open a window to the sentiments on the street that can be elusive even for an intelligence service as pervasive as the one in Syria. There is an added advantage, explained Amiralay. "From the beginning of the Assad era, they created this margin; you have a way to let off the steam, like a pressure cooker."

But I did not understand the logic of repression. The harshest crackdown on the fledgling reform movement in Syria came in 2006. By then, Bashar al-Assad had gained not only breathing room domestically but also outside advocates for his continued rule. Even the Israelis had counseled Washington to show restraint in shaking the Assad regime. I asked Amiralay why the Syrian authorities cracked down on a weakened reform movement, with little support from the Syrian population, at a time when the regime was sure of its staying power.

"They are more repressive when they are strong, to show to the foreign powers that we don't give up. This is the message. We repress our people even if we don't need to. Even when there is a minimum of resistance, they will eliminate it—just to prove that they are strong enough not to give in to Washington's pressure. They take the country hostage to prove that they have the right politics and have taken the right decisions."

In a country as highly fragmented as Syria, with the danger that sectarianism could cross the border from Iraq, and a hostile administration in Washington, Bashar al-Assad's government had determined it could not afford to show weakness. Bashar consolidated his power, weakened the opposition, and offered Syrians the consolation of an opening in the economy—symbolized by a rush of new business opportunities, computers, new cars, and cheap imported consumer goods. The unemployment rate still hovered at 20 percent, even higher for the young. The corruption among the ruling elite, and especially in the circle of family and loyalists surrounding the president, was as rapacious as ever. But for the average Syrian, health care was free, gas was subsidized, and food was still relatively cheap. Syria was calm. While this purchasing of domestic quiet might represent a short-term strategy, in the Middle East it counted as successful ruling politics.

Amiralay considered Syria's future as daylight faded on the tree-lined street in Damascus. We had been sitting in the courtyard of an art gallery for a couple of hours, resupplied with glasses of tea in keeping with the dictates of Damascene hospitality. "Syrian society is suffering," he said. "I mean we are completely underdeveloped in science and medicine." The collapse of Syria's reform movement meant that Bashar and his committed lieutenants would dictate the pace of change. Had Bashar survived because Syrian policy was the right one for this time or because the Bush administration made so many mistakes in the region? Amiralay had been asking himself the same question. "They know, the Syrian regime knows, they survived because there is a disaster in the Middle East. Bashar is not a passive player. He did everything to make things worse around him. He interfered in Lebanon, in Iraq, and in Palestine." And Bashar, like his father, got away with it. Hafez al-Assad invented a method of maneuvering his small, economically weak but strategically placed country into a power broker's role by making alliances and issuing threats with equal vigor. Today, his son's immediate goal is to preserve the rule of his Alawite regime in a Sunni-dominated country.

For Amiralay, there were many guilty parties responsible for the mess in the region. Iraq was just one example. But the problem was so much bigger than Iraq and it was here, in a strange confluence of ideas, that Amiralay, a longtime dissident and former Marxist, shared some of the sentiments of the most stalwart supporters of George W. Bush. The authoritarian rulers in the region were the problem, that was the correct diagnosis, but Washington's method for dealing with them had been a disaster. "Bush [was] the fruitcake, in the middle of the wedding confection," explained Amiralay, smiling as he pictured the image he had created to make this so simple even an American could understand. "The whole cake is the problem. But Bush, he was a little piece of this problem."

The region's longterm autocrats could now link Iraq to the American project in the Middle East. Democracy and pluralism had become a much harder sell.

CHAPTER SIX

"THE MOST HONEST HOUSEWIFE IN THE WORLD"

Um Nour was not pleased. I could see her eyes tighten slightly as she surveyed my attire. Not pleased. She pursed her lips and reached into her handbag for a bottle of strong flowery perfume and rubbed it over my hands.

A Sunni woman who had run from death threats in a Shiite neighborhood in Baghdad, Um Nour was pretty and pale, a single mother, well upholstered, who had come to Damascus in 2006. When we first met, she had welcomed me into her modest home on the bottom floor of an unfinished concrete apartment block in a neighborhood crowded with refugee families. We had talked for a couple of hours, stretched out in her daughter's bedroom like old friends. She had been remarkably candid about the prevalence of prostitution in the exile community. The conversation ended when her two children, a teenaged daughter and a somewhat younger son, came home from school and Um Nour resumed her role as an affectionate, protective mother.

A few months earlier, she had offered to take me to her favorite nightclub. "You won't have to pay any money to go there," she assured me. But Um Nour was in charge of the evening and I had to pass her careful inspection. I had rummaged through my traveling wardrobe for something appropriate. An alluring nightclub outfit was going to be a stretch. She looked through my cosmetics bag and decided that what I lacked in exposed cleavage could be offset by an Iraqi-style application of makeup. By way of advice, she gave me one firm warning: "Don't speak English."

Um Nour's invitation would help me answer a question I had struggled with: Why had so many Iraqi women and girls turned to the sex trade for survival in Damascus? That question led to more questions, including: Why wasn't anyone doing much to protect them? I had interviewed experts at the office of the United Nations High Commissioner for Refugees and talked to dozens of Iraqi exiles, but to interview the women and girls who make a living in the sex trade, to spend time with them, was more difficult than I imagined. Um Nour was my best chance for getting a look inside the business and she was willing to take me there.

Each time I returned to Damascus during 2008, I made a point of seeing Um Nour. Prostitution among refugees was another fallout from the Iraq war, and her choice of this survival strategy in Damascus was a measure of the welfare of the exile community. Over time her life had improved. She could now afford the school fees for her children, and on one visit I noticed new furniture in the front room of her apartment. She served tea there to celebrate her rising affluence.

On yet another visit, she volunteered shyly that she had two lovers. I assumed that these men provided some of her income. She offered the barest details of her personal life, instead steering my questions to the conditions affecting the broader community. The price of food was rising, she told me. Life was hard for everyone. Jobs were scarce. But despite the hardships Iraqi exiles were not going back to Baghdad yet. She was not going back to Baghdad. She vowed to stay in Damascus until the Shiite-dominated government changed in Iraq.

Um Nour never admitted she was a prostitute, and I never asked her the question directly. Our conversations about the sex trade in Damascus remained on "Iraqi" terms, vague on her personal involvement and on the moral dilemma, but specific on the details of what other women did. Um Nour's stories about herself were filled with omissions; but then, selective recall is a survival skill.

It was difficult for Iraqi women to acknowledge such shameful behavior. In all of my interviews only one woman told me directly how she raised money to support her children and the rest of her family. "I go with men," Hiba said bluntly. We were sitting in her apartment, in her daughter's bedroom. Hiba's mother was sitting beside her and had just told me that Hiba worked as a house cleaner. But Hiba, a pretty twenty-seven-year-old, rolled her eyes and snorted at her mother's bald-faced lie.

Hiba's calculated candor made her mother cross her arms and look away.

"In Baghdad, I was the most honest housewife in the world," she asserted, more for her mother's approval than for mine. Hiba told me that she had graduated from college, then married and become a full-time mother after her first daughter was born. Her father had been a goldsmith, and the family had lived comfortably in Iraq. Hiba and her family are Mandaeans, a religious minority that is among Iraq's oldest, predating Christianity and Islam. Mandaeans revere John the Baptist, and their religious rituals, from baptisms to weddings, are performed in the muddy waters of Iraq's Tigris River. The community's wealth and faith placed them at risk from Islamic radicals. In Saddam's time, about seventy thousand Mandaeans lived in Iraq; by 2008, almost all of them had fled the country.

In 2004, Hiba's daughter was kidnapped when the family was on an outing to visit relatives, "and the gangsters were following us," she explained. The family raised a $20,000 ransom, but soon after Hiba's daughter was returned, they were threatened again because of their religion. The extended family fled to Syria in 2005.

A full-lipped woman with large eyes and shiny brown hair, Hiba waved her two young daughters out of the room. Hiba said she was now the sole wage earner for the family after her husband had disappeared eight months earlier. "He felt so tired of living. He ran away." Her story trailed off. Was this the event that had pushed Hiba into the sex trade? Or did her husband walk out the door because of Hiba's work? I couldn't help wondering as I looked around the small well-furnished apartment. There was a television in the living room and another one in the girls' bedroom alongside a DVD player. There were balloons on the living room carpet, left over from a birthday party for her daughters the day before. Hiba wore a heavy gold necklace that spelled her name in large English letters. A small diamond glittered on one letter.

Hiba spoke openly about her "work" three nights a week. She went to "parties" in a neighborhood outside Damascus known as a center for prostitution. Working at arranged parties meant Hiba could stay out of the seedy nightclub circuit. These apartment parties were a more private corner of the sex trade.

"Men go there and the men drink and dance and get drunk," Hiba told me. "Then, they choose me. This place is for this purpose. Bad friends took me there."

How much can you make, I asked gently. She sighed. "Fifty dollars, if I am there for the party and if I don't go with somebody—if I do, then it's one hundred dollars."

I wanted to know about the other women, Iraqi women. Had she become friendly with the others there?

"The families bring them. All of their families know what they are doing. Some even bring their brothers with them. The other girls, they don't like me. They think I'm arrogant. They are surprised when they find out I am from a good family. Nobody wants to be doing this, but it's the only way."

"Even to go and sit in this place and do nothing is bad for me. The wave there is high. I could be taken in." I figured that the wave Hiba was talking about was the wave of despair, giving up on the future and resigning herself to a career in the sex trade in Damascus. I had no doubt that she had already been touched by that wave. Each question Hiba answered landed like a blow on her mother, who listened silently throughout. Had they discussed the options before Hiba took the first job? Or did this lively young woman, abandoned by her husband, simply decide to attend a "party," a simulation of normal life? When she walked away with cash in hand at the end of the evening, did she wonder how she would feel the second time, the third, the one-hundredth time?

Hiba wanted me to know that she was a good woman, an educated woman, who had been forced to make a sacrifice that had weighed on her more heavily than on the rest of the family. "Sometimes I remember the good days. We had a big house, I had servants at home." She dabbed at her eyes for the first time in more than an hour of conversation. "All of that has gone with Iraq. Bush took everything."

I asked Um Nour one evening if women like Hiba could ever go back to Iraq.

"Here in Syria, they know us. I would be killed if I went back. Immediately killed by my relatives," Um Nour said, slipping into the first person because I had hit on a particularly sensitive subject. Prostitution is a special taboo for Arab women because the shame extends to the entire family and can lead to so-called honor killings by male relatives.

"I know other girls who say this, too," she said. "Some of the girls wear *nekab* on the stage to make sure they don't see anyone they know."

Um Nour explained that *nekab*, the black face-veil usually worn by conservative Muslim women, was a tool of concealment for prostitutes on the dance stage, a hopeful protection against the surprise of a male relative or old neighbor among the patrons. Um Nour had mentioned the face-veil before, in our first meeting, when she described the costumes worn at the nightclub. She was scathing about the young girls who wore next to nothing when they paraded onstage, but reserved her harshest criticism for the women who danced in *nekab*. At the time, I thought she was commenting on her disdain for the hypocrisy of seemingly religiously observant women who had gotten into the trade. But this was another cultural lesson altogether. For Um Nour, *nekab* was a reminder that she had chosen a survival strategy that would preclude her future return to Iraq. In another story, I had heard about an Iraqi woman in the sex trade whose clients were young Shiite men from the Mahdi militia who came to Syria in the summer for vacation. They paid her for sex, enjoyed her company, but threatened that if she ever came back to Baghdad they would cut her head off.

Hundreds, perhaps thousands, of the Iraqi exiles in Syria had turned to the sex trade for survival. Nearly every war brings prostitution. But in Damascus, girls as young as ten were forced into the trade by parents—fathers or mothers, who made the deal and lived off the proceeds. Officially, refugees were not permitted to hold jobs and had to manage on whatever savings they had. As resources dwindled, despair and desperation set in, which led some to the underground economy.

Female-headed households accounted for almost a quarter of the refugees registered with the United Nations refugee agency. Widowed, divorced, or separated from husbands by the war, many women had children or elderly parents to support. Sex was often their only marketable asset.

With the thriving trade in low-priced Iraqi prostitutes, many of them young girls, Damascus became a destination for sex tourism, competing with the brothels of Lebanon.

"One place is called Saudi street," explained Asir Madaien, a short, compact Jordanian woman who was a protection officer at the United Nations High Commissioner for Refugees based in Damascus. The "street" was a section of the city where Saudi men rented vacation apartments and then negotiated for companionship.

"These Saudis pay $5,000 for a month with a girl. The Gulfies propose the deal to the mother. A lot of the deals are done by cellphone. Some of the Kuwaitis say they come here because this is their revenge on Saddam." At this last detail, Asir raised her eyebrows and cocked her head to make sure I understood the significance.

The animosity between Iraq and Kuwait did involve sex, prostitution, and the price of oil. During his televised trial in Baghdad, Saddam Hussein became especially agitated when the discussion turned to Iraq's 1990 invasion of Kuwait, one of the broad charges the Iraqi judge read out in the courtroom.

"How could Saddam be tried over Kuwait," Saddam had thundered, referring to himself in the third person. "How could you defend those dogs? They were trying to turn Iraqi women into ten-dinar prostitutes," he shouted at the judge. Ten-dinar prostitutes—this was an old hurt. Many Iraqis also believed that in the 1990s the Kuwaitis had intentionally reduced the price of oil to squeeze Iraqi's economy after the devastating Iran-Iraq war. The "trying to turn Iraqi women into ten-dinar prostitutes" line was an insult reportedly delivered by the emir of Kuwait during a crucial meeting with Iraq's foreign minister. After the American invasion, in his jail cell, Saddam had confided to an FBI agent that this was the reason he had ordered the invasion of Kuwait. Every Iraqi already knew the story. The animosity between Iraq and Kuwait outlasted Saddam.

"Not all of them do it willingly. The husbands threaten. Often a woman will get married just to get out of Iraq and then will be forced into prostitution when she gets here," said Asir Madaien. A UNHCR program to protect vulnerable Iraqi women was put in place only in 2007. Asir had less access to the women who worked in the sex trade than I did.

"The youngest I've seen is twelve years. I saw two men from the Gulf, with these young girls, they were together at seven A.M. in the morning." Asir was dropping off her own children at school when she caught sight of the two men in long white *thobes*, the distinctive male dress of the Gulf. As a UN official she wasn't allowed to visit the night-clubs, but she had set up an outreach program, hiring forty Iraqi female refugees to identify cases.

"We also find them in the juvenile rehabilitation centers. Some-times the Syrian police arrest the girls they find in an apartment, sometimes seven or eight at a time, all under the age of thirteen." But for these young Iraqi girls the odds of improving their prospects were poor.

"We offer assistance. We can hand over cash, $200 a month. But the families say, 'We can get this in one day, so why should we stop,'" she added, a note of frustration rising in her voice. "We have a problem in reaching out to the families. Even when you get a girl released, and the family is involved, she will soon disappear."

Asir shook her head. She was struggling to comprehend how parents—fathers or mothers—could exploit their daughters. She had worked with Iraqi refugees in Jordan and Syria. She began by explaining that this was now a part of Iraqi culture, the result of complex factors including Saddam Hussein's destruction of the Iraqi character, the United Nations sanctions, the American occupation, and the constant violence. The numerous explanations seemed to add up to some kind of post-Saddam traumatic disorder. But I had met many Iraqis who loved their children and protected them, even in the harshest conditions of exile. I knew many Iraqi women in Damascus who found other ways to support their families. Asir finally settled on an all-embracing summation for the shocking behavior of desperate people. "We have learned over time that Iraqis have lost hope. They don't believe in a future any longer. They have become survivors."

Um Nour checked her watch. It was close to midnight and she wanted to get to the nightclub so we could spend the rest of the evening there. Although I had failed the dress test, Um Nour's transformation was remarkable. I would not have recognized her on the street. In our daytime meetings, she dressed in baggy track pants, black hair tied back in a ponytail, her face lined and tired. Now, her long black hair was shiny and brushed with thick bangs that framed her face. She wore a tight-fitting black T-shirt sprinkled with sequins and black stretch pants tightly cinched at the waist. Her lipstick was deep red, her eyeliner heavy and black. She wore two rhinestone rings, her stubby fingers extended by fake red nails curled around an expensive cellphone.

Um Nour escorted me into the club, past men in black dinner jackets at the front door. Syrians owned the club, paid off the Syrian police when necessary, and called them in when there was trouble. Most of the clientele were Iraqis. The room was vast and dark, with spotlights trained on the dance stage. A live band played somewhere in the gloom behind the stage, making conversation almost impossible. There were at least a hundred tables. Most of the customers sat in small groups near the stage, drinking watered *arak* and Johnnie Walker, sipping in the low haze of smoke from apple-infused tobacco in bubbling water pipes. Family groups sat farther back: mothers, fathers, and young daughters. Single women in their twenties and thirties had claimed seats in the darkest places, the better to survey the room. Um Nour picked a table near the back entrance, secured our spot, and gestured to the ladies' restroom. We had gotten past the Syrian owners, but I would have to fit in with the mostly Iraqi clientele.

"I will never dance until I get so drunk," said a woman in a pink latex jumpsuit with clear-plastic shoulder straps that kept the tight fabric in place. She was bent toward the mirror in the ladies' room, applying eyeliner, next to a line of Iraqi women in the same pose. It was an utterly familiar female ritual: women gathering in front of a public bathroom mirror. It could have been anywhere, but for the outfits of tight fabrics and silver spandex revealing tactile, soft, full breasts served up for inspection. Clinging fabric over ample round backsides. Long skirts, slit to the thigh, bellies exposed. Gleaming black hair. High-heeled boots. Young faces. Curvaceous bodies. One last look? Enough eyeliner? Another pat of powder? Anxiety also filled the room, because of the deals that would have to be concluded later in the evening. One woman, maybe twenty but probably younger, was dressed as a school-girl. As we all prepared for the night ahead, the Iraqi women chatted, traded names and phone numbers. They flipped open cellphones and showed the pictures of their young children. Lingering together in this comfortable female place, homesick, they were preparing to live off their bodies.

Another woman said her name was Abeer. "My husband tried to smuggle the kids to Sweden, but they got caught and are back in Baghdad," she told me. She had divorced her husband when he set off for Sweden. She had agreed to the separation for the sake of her two children. Now, she lived with her sister, and worried about her kids. She sent her club earnings home for them. But why had she come to Damascus, I asked; what had driven her to come here in the first place? "I was a journalist," she said. In 2007, she was hired by a television station based in Baghdad. She worked as a correspondent until the day her mother found a letter that had been thrown into the family garden: "Leave in 48 hours or we will kill you." Syria was the only open border. While I was pondering Abeer's choices, she clicked her cellphone shut, took one last look at her mirror image, and moved toward to door. "Have a good night," she said knowingly, one businesswoman to another, as she made her way into the dark nightclub.

I could see why this was Um Nour's favorite club. The system of cost-and-rewards favored women who wanted some control over their work. It was a freelance market. We had walked in through the front door for "free," while the male patrons paid a steep cover charge and even more for the alcohol and snacks delivered to the table. Um Nour explained that women paid the Syrian men at the door at the end of the night—but only if they left with a man.

Iraq has a long historical connection to prostitution. The Whore of Babylon is a character in the Bible's Book of Revelations, the symbol of all things evil. The world's oldest profession was first recorded in Mesopotamia in the second millennium B.C. The code of Hammurabi, the ancient world's first fixed laws for a metropolis, acknowledged prostitution and gave prostitutes some inheritance rights. But Iraq's modern dictator, Saddam Hussein, had set the stage for the moral decline of his population.

That he did so came as no surprise even to the Iraqis I knew who were most disturbed by the rampant prostitution among the exile community. Many had lived in Baghdad when prostitution was public. At the close of the Iran-Iraq war, prostitutes, protected by the regime, were encouraged to welcome the returning troops—a benevolent "victory present" from Saddam. In the 1990s, another time of hopelessness, prostitution became more widespread. The United Nations sanctions, imposed in 1991 to force Saddam to reveal and destroy Iraq's suspected weapons of mass destruction, ushered in a decade of deprivation and corruption. Saddam was unmoved by the punishing financial and trade embargo, but ordinary Iraqis were impoverished, humbled by destitution, as the social fabric of the country unraveled. I had heard many stories about these years. Iraqis poured out searing memories that were as clear and important as the current U.S. occupation. "My father always said one Bush starved us, the other Bush drove us from our homes," as an Iraqi doctor put it. His wealthy father had been ruined by the UN embargo, which reduced the family's daily diet to tomatoes, bread, and onions, with small bits of meat for special occasions. Even the most common illnesses, previously treatable, could be a death sentence as medical supplies dried up. An Iraqi actor told me his bitterest memories came from the sanctions decade as his father moved the large family to cheaper and cheaper accommodations and his sister died prematurely due to inadequate medical care. In those desperate times, Iraqi women had also turned to prostitution to survive.

Another friend who had lived in Baghdad throughout this period observed: "You cannot overestimate the damage those sanctions did to the society. It was a casual thing for an Iraqi brother to help his sister, escorting her to a paying customer because it was improper for her to go alone. University students engaged in prostitution because they needed the cash for food. The administrative staff at the universities would take the role of pimps." Iraqis keenly recalled not only the social wreckage but also the period in the 1990s when Saddam turned to Islam to shore up his legitimacy and suddenly acquired a new moral censoriousness.

Saddam's national faith campaign had singled out prostitutes and included a public campaign to halt their activities. Appearing on Iraqi television, Saddam announced that these Iraqi women "were dishonoring their country." Between 2000 and 2001, he unleashed the Feda'iyye Saddam, a militia created by his son, Uday, to send an unmistakable message to a beaten-down population. Women accused of prostitution were rounded up and publicly beheaded in Baghdad and in other cities. The executioners carried out their work with swords. The severed heads of the condemned women were left on the doorsteps of their homes. Honor is a deeply held concept in Iraqi identity and women play a significant role. The horrific beheadings, the public humiliation of entire families, amplified Saddam's cruelty and turned the punishment into a state-sanctioned desecration of a family's name. But in the moral landscape of exile—shaped, in part, by Iraq's sectarian civil war—honor was abandoned in the struggle to survive.

I would have to dance. In the dark at the back of the room the stage seemed like a bright planet, a place so distant I could barely make out the life forms. Um Nour had left me sitting alone. She was wandering around the club, greeting old friends. She had explained to the group of men sitting behind us that I was Ukrainian and therefore didn't speak Arabic, but that didn't stop them from sending drinks to the table and trying to engage me in drunken conversation. When one kissed me on the top of my head, I decided that I'd be safer on stage.

I climbed up into the bright lights. Most of the dancers seemed alone in the crowd. An older woman, in a simple red dress more appropriate for a day at the market, had been on the dance floor all night. She appeared to be listening to music from some distant time inside her head; eyes closed, she mouthed the lyrics of traditional laments of loss. With each refrain, her eyes moistened and she took the cigarette she was holding and brought the burning tip close to the exposed skin above her breasts. Over and over she brought the smoldering tobacco near her naked skin, about to inflict pain, but stopping short of contact. When the music ended she left the stage for a refresher of tobacco and alcohol.

Two girls danced together, fingers locked, madly twirling waist-long dark hair in circles to the beat of the music. One of them I recognized from the ladies' room; no longer wearing her schoolgirl's outfit, she had changed into a still more revealing costume and had paired herself with another long-haired beauty. Were they a package deal? Did they even know each other? They embraced like old friends but did not make eye contact with each other or with any other dancer on the stage. Beside them were two little girls, no more than twelve years old, in party dresses and lipstick. They copied the faces of the older women on stage—giddy, shiny-faced dancers at three o'clock in the morning.

The undeclared rules of the dance floor segregated the dancers. Men danced with men, arms entwined over shoulders, in short lines, flinging out one leg at a time and moving in a circle. Women danced alone or in pairs. Breaking the rules, pairing a man and a woman, would imply a business arrangement, and it was too early in the evening for that. The men mounted the stage to scout, to get a better look at the merchandise on offer.

The entertainment was tailored to an Iraqi audience, the music a medley of emotional, nostalgic old favorites from home. A comedian pumped up the audience by calling out the names of Iraqi cities. Baghdad! Sulemaniyah! Mosul! The applause built for each constituency. He told jokes about the hard life in Damascus and played to the overwhelming longing for home. Then the band struck up another familiar tune and the next singer started the first few words of a song the audience knew well, a song of praise for Saddam. A blue laser light shot out from the audience and tapped the singer's face. In mid-lyric, he switched to a tribute to the Iraqi national football team, eliciting widespread applause and calming the crowd of drunken men.

Abeer discovered me on the dance floor. I hadn't seen her since our conversation in the ladies' room. She wanted a dance partner and we were now old friends. She grabbed my hand and I was grateful. What choice was there? I was out of place, uncomfortable, a little scared in this crowd. My limited Arabic would not get me out of trouble. I needed a friend and Abeer had offered her hand, a partner for my charade. We danced. We rolled our eyes at the little girls on the stage as they became clumsy and tired and knocked into the other dancers. The red lady with the cigarettes was still with us and we shook our heads and wondered what trauma she was playing out. We moved around the dance floor, took in the details, looked at the faces, and then I saw Nezar Hussein, my translator and friend.

He was dancing, too, arms tangled in a line of men, smiling broadly when I finally noticed him. Unknown to me, he had been at the club all night, sitting across the room, my silent protector. I was relieved to see him. We made a plan to meet at the back entrance and share a cab for the trip home to compare notes on the rest of the dancers.

The man in the black dinner jacket at the front door demanded 500 Syrian liras, equivalent to about $15. He stretched out his hand and looked at me. He wanted his commission. I was leaving with a man, albeit Nezar, and I was now expected to pay up out of my expected proceeds. "But he's my friend!" I said blurting it out in English, momentarily forgetting Um Nour's instruction. Nezar and I had walked out together, reclaiming our identities at the front door, but to the Syrian controllers we were still part of the nightclub clientele. The dinner jacket stretched out his hand again and repeated, more forcefully this time, his demand for a cut of the deal. Five hundred, he said. We kept walking toward the cab and he watched us go. "Don't ever come back here again," he said glaring. That was easy. I did not ever want to come back again. The undertow of despair was too great.

In the taxi, Nezar and I marveled at the dancer in the red dress, the cigarette lady, who had sat out the intermissions on Nezar's side of the room. "I saw her beating herself every time the singer started a song about mothers. She beat her breast really hard. When she saw me watching her, she came over to my chair and kissed me on my eyes. And she was crying." We both shook our heads at the unimaginable calamity. We were tired, emotionally exhausted, and completely sober.

"I saw Um Nour showing pictures on her mobile phone," said Nezar. He had saved this detail for last. "I mean, I wasn't far from her when she came to my side of the room. Photos of almost-naked girls," he said. Um Nour was a madam? She was trafficking young girls when she got up from the table and circulated among the male customers in the club? She was tough, a survivor. I should not have been so surprised. Each time I had asked her about her own daughter Um Nour had proudly answered that both of her children were in school. She was making sure they had a good future. Her children were Iraqis and one day they could go home.

CHAPTER SEVEN

LEBANON'S IRAQ WAR

For Iraqis who could not abide the heavy hand of the Syrian regime, the lightly governed system of Lebanon became an alternative destination. Some fifty thousand Iraqi refugees had collected there by 2009. The official total was just a guess. While some Iraqi exiles entered the country legally, mingling at the airport with the tourist crowds from the Gulf, many more entered the country illegally. Smugglers brought them west, from the Syrian border, over the mountain trails in the north. Many had made the last miles of the journey on foot. In Beirut, I met a middle-aged librarian from Mosul, a Christian grandmother who had been threatened by Islamic militants. She had carried her two young grandsons on her back, walking for hours on dirt roads in the mountains after dark on her way to Beirut.

The journey to Lebanon was often riskier than to Damascus, but the prohibition against work was more relaxed and Lebanon's sectarian system worked to the advantage of the new arrivals. In Lebanon, sectarian politics were on full display, but this Mediterranean pluralism offered a safe haven for most refugees as soon as they arrived.

Young, single Iraqi Shiite men headed for Beirut's Shiite enclave south of the capital. Protected by Hezbollah, the Iraqis joined construction crews to rebuild the Lebanese neighborhoods destroyed by Israeli bombs in 2006—refugees from one war ended up repairing the wreckage of another. Iraqi Christians, about 30 percent of the exiles in Lebanon, could count on help from the Assyrian and Chaldean churches. Wealthy Iraqi Sunnis rented apartments in the predominantly Sunni neighborhoods of West Beirut; the poor headed to Tripoli, Lebanon's Sunni city in the north. The exiles aggravated Lebanon's sectarian divide. How much so would depend on how long they stayed. Lebanon had the lowest number of refugees registered by the United Nations High Commissioner for Refugees office, suggesting that many Iraqis who came to Lebanon did not register because they considered the country only a temporary retreat.

But there was another group of exiles, self-defined Iraqi refugees, jihadi salafist militants, who were the losers in a sectarian war in Iraq. They were not welcome in their countries of origin. These were the Arab fighters, Sunni jihadis, the veterans of the anti-U.S. insurgency in Iraq. They could not legally cross international borders because their names were on Interpol lists. Lebanon was the safe haven of last resort because the central state was weak and border controls lax. The fighters, too, could expect sectarian shelter and safety in a country where radicalism and religious fervor had been accelerated by events in Iraq.

Since the early days of the war in Iraq, traffic at the porous Lebanese border had been two-way, much of it over mountain paths where smuggling is one of the main local industries. Even before Iraqi refugees streamed west into Lebanon, militant young men—Lebanese and other Arabs—headed east, following the jihadi trails to enlist in Iraq's growing insurgency. The Lebanese militants came from the miserable neighborhoods of Tripoli in the north, the Sunni farming villages in the eastern Bekaa Valley, and the country's teeming Palestinian refugee camps. All were fertile recruiting grounds for "martyrdom operations" on the Iraqi battlefield.

Abu Musab al-Zarqawi, the Jordanian Islamist who formed Al Qaeda in Mesopotamia, openly recruited in Lebanon's Sunni mosques in 2004. The comfortable Lebanese merchants of the capital didn't seem to notice when the survivors came back to Lebanon as hardened veterans trained in urban warfare. Most of the country reacted with surprise and alarm when militants waged a military campaign from inside a refugee camp that threatened the security of Lebanon's fragile state in the summer of 2007. Fatah al Islam, a Sunni militia that claimed links with Al Qaeda, had slipped into the country unnoticed until a showdown with the Lebanese army became a national crisis and gave every Lebanese a stake in the outcome.

Major General Ashraf Rifi, the head of Lebanon's Internal Security Forces (ISF), kicked off a war with Fatah al Islam on May 20, 2007. The battle turned into a siege, lasting more than a hundred days and costing more than three hundred lives, fourty-two of them civilians. Fatah al Islam was defeated but the presence of Al Qaeda–linked groups was not eliminated. Lebanon was a new front for radical groups who adopted the tactics and ideology of Al Qaeda.

Major General Rifi was celebrating his fifty-fourth birthday the day I met him in Beirut. An officer in a decorated beige uniform juggled two large cakes past my place on the reception room couch—one garnished with ruby-red cherries glistening with sugar, the other covered in thick dark chocolate. Lebanese security officers filed into Rifi's office and wished him a long life. It is a meaningful wish in a building with heavy blast doors that seal off the secure areas and a wall lined with Lebanese flags and the pictures of officers who have been blown up for carrying out their duties. A Lebanese pop star, Raghad Alami, a sculpted and styled head among the close-cropped cuts, had come to sing the birthday song. Dressed in designer jeans and with a brilliant whitened smile, Alami looked wildly out of place at a policeman's party. After the short celebration, he walked out through the reception room where I was waiting and, reflexively thrusting out his hand for a strong shake, answered a question I had not asked: "We hope to fight terrorism together!" A pop-cop alliance was an odd and unlikely response to the fact that a war in Iraq had spilled into Lebanon.

Major General Rifi, a balding man, trim in a uniform sporting rows of shiny medals, with the jaded demeanor of a big-city police chief, had decided that since he was talking to a foreign journalist he would give a speech emphasizing the positives, much of which were utterly inconsequential. He began by directing my attention to Lebanon's crime record. "Just to give you an example, for the whole of Lebanon, we have seventeen murders a month," he told me, reading from a chart he had prepared. "And then there are times when the political situation is different and this can go higher. So, in normal times, Lebanon is stable," he said, offering what he considered numerical proof that four million Lebanese citizens were not naturally violent people. The comforting statistics ignored the historical record of Lebanon's fifteen-year civil war. In Rifi's version, the country's rate of untimely deaths was actually quite low considering Lebanon's socioeconomic disparities and sectarian tensions. He went on to suggest that Lebanon was in general blameless and that, in the logic of anxious nation-states everywhere, whatever problems did exist stemmed from the neighbors.

"So, terrorism is not a natural phenomenon in Lebanon; it comes from outside or it is to do with external politics." Rifi, an intelligent, rational man on police matters, was out of his depth in the murkier waters of politics.

Outside players have been a part of Lebanon's political landscape throughout the country's modern history, a practice that continued after 1943, when Lebanon gained its independence from France. Lebanon's major sects—Sunnis, Shiites, and Christians—all had powerful outside patrons. Over the years Iran, Syria, France, and Saudi Arabia, as well as the United States, had taken part in proxy wars on Lebanese soil. Lebanese officials often blamed outside powers for the country's troubles, but did not often acknowledge that Lebanese politicians invited outsiders in to strengthen a weak political hand. As long as Lebanon's constitution divided influence by religious faction, and as long as those factions received significant external assistance and support—military, political, and economic—the center was not going to be able to hold the idea of a unified country. It was too readily subject to the larger politics of the region and the shifting interests of Lebanon's regional and international patrons.

Mindful of the empowerment of the Shiites in Iraq, the Shiites of Lebanon more forcefully asserted that they were the single largest sectarian group in Lebanon, underrepresented and owed a fairer share of power at the expense of the dominant Sunnis and the powerful Christian minority. Also mindful of the similar showdown, Al Qaeda–affiliated groups in Lebanon claimed to be guardians of Sunni interests and identity in a repeat of the strategy that had wreaked such havoc in Iraq.

Outside powers lined up along Sunni-Shiite lines. Iran and Syria supported the Shiites versus a Western alliance led by the United States that also included the region's Sunni powerhouse, Saudi Arabia. The relatively unknown Al Qaeda–affiliated Fatah al Islam was a new ingredient, one that generated a menu of contradicting conspiracy theories about outside and inside backers. According to some observers, Syria had recruited the militants from Syrian jails to destabilize the Lebanese government. Others believed that Lebanon's Sunni politicians had funded and promoted the radical Sunni militia as a means of countering the Shiite militia of Hezbollah—or that the

Americans and the Saudis were Fatah al Islam's paymasters. Each of the opposing theories was endlessly debated and, like all good conspiracy stories, contained some kernels of truth but neglected the wider implications.

Rifi insisted that the men who had come to organize Fatah al Islam were "Syrians, Palestinians, a small number of Saudis, Algerians, Chechen, and in my opinion, they were here for a mission in Lebanon. They came out of Iraq for this." There were Lebanese, too, but Rifi was not quick to recognize this fact in his account.

It was hard to know exactly when the Iraqi war spilled over into Lebanon, or exactly when Arab and Iraqi fighters had infiltrated into the Palestinian refugee camps of Lebanon. There was no doubt these committed militants had taken up residence in the warren-like neighborhoods of Lebanon's decades-old refugee camps. The dozen camps had long been a sanctuary for wanted men.

The tightly packed ghettos were a no-go zone for the Lebanese army and security services because of a 1969 agreement ceding security responsibility to the Palestine Liberation Organization. However, in recent years, the dissolving discipline of Palestinian nationalism was losing out to a more muscular, globalized jihadi movement that was part of the Sunni Islamist revival sweeping Lebanon and the region, with Al Qaeda's ideology being the most radical form.

Among Lebanon's Palestinians, young, third-generation refugees had lost hope in liberating Palestine and found a more promising cause in the mujahedeen in Bosnia, Chechnya, Afghanistan, and then Iraq— all places where they had gone to fight. It was hardly surprising that jihadi veterans from the Iraq campaign would end up in these camps or that new jihadi volunteers would be derived from those who lived there seemingly permanently.

Signing up to a global movement was one way to counter the impotence of life in the Palestinian camps, according to French scholar

Bernard Rougier, an expert on jihadist movements in Lebanon. "Palestinian salafist militants have devoted themselves to defending the imaginary borders of identity," Rougier had written, "declaring themselves the protectors and the guardians of the cause of Sunni Islam worldwide." Rougier was in Lebanon to observe the latest developments in northern Lebanon, and when we talked about the emergence of Fatah al Islam, he explained: "The way of solving the contradiction of being in Lebanon but not fighting Israel or anybody else is by sending jihadists to Iraq and supporting groups like Fatah al Islam." Rougier flat-out disagreed with Rifi, so I asked the Lebanese security chief why he thought it had been so easy for Fatah al Islam to set up a training base in northern Lebanon and to offer refuge to foreign fighters, Iraqis, and other Arabs when they left Iraq.

Rifi finally began talking about the Lebanese, the young Sunni fundamentalists, the religiously fervent men of Tripoli. They were the first recruits of Fatah al Islam. "Fatah al Islam said they were a jihadi movement, and some of the guys believed it and joined." It was an unusually frank acknowledgment that Lebanon had its own share of homegrown Sunni Islamists well known to the Internal Security Forces. Tripoli was a good place to grow them.

The largest city in northern Lebanon, Tripoli, known as Lebanon's "Sunni capital," is a conservative Muslim city, its economic development long ignored by Beirut politicians. "Certainly there is a lot of anger in the poorer areas. That is where people tend to go toward extremism, in the poorer areas," said Rifi. He knew Tripoli well. It was his hometown; his family lived there and he commuted to his job in Beirut. Tripoli was a radical town with black banners on traffic islands whose inscriptions supported a radical version of jihad, or holy war. In the poorest neighborhood, a large billboard with Saddam's picture declared that his death was a sectarian lynching rather than an execution after a legal proceeding carried out by the authority of the Iraqi government. In the dark hallways of Tripoli's predominantly Sunni slum neighborhoods, graffiti on the walls proclaimed Osama bin Laden as "our" leader. "The strongest anger was in Tripoli," Rifi confirmed. "Of course, the Sunnis were affected not only by Iraq but by Palestine, and these situations pumped them up. They became very aggressive."

The 2003 U.S. invasion of Iraq fanned the long-burning flame, giving the angry young men of Tripoli an outlet for venting their rage. When they came home from the anti-U.S. jihad in Iraq, the Lebanese fighters brought comrades with them and found refuge in Lebanon's Palestinian camps, which remained off-limits to the police and the army. In this way, the unintended consequences of a generation of exiles that began in 1948 contributed to the ongoing destabilization of the region and the creation of a newly displaced people. It was a perfect example of the cost of doing nothing to solve an earlier refugee crisis: Ignore it for long enough and it will fan the next crisis and seed future ones.

The Lebanese army assault on Fatah al Islam began on May 20, 2007, a siege that destroyed the buildings and barracks of the Nahr al Barid refugee camp and devastated the lives of the Palestinian civilians living there. But the militant community with a longer history of radicalism stayed out of the fight. Ain el-Helweh, a Palestinian refugee camp near the coastal town of Sidon, about an hour's drive south of Beirut, was also a haven for jihadi refugees from Iraq. Radicals in the refugee camp had more direct links to Al Qaeda. Arab and European intelligence agencies had listening posts in the nearby town of Sidon to keep watch and track cellphone communications. As Bernard Rougier pointed out in his study of Ain el-Helweh, "a video aired by al-Qaeda in September 2006 showed a young Saudi—one of the nineteen operatives who died on September 11—dedicating a poem to 'Abu Mahjin the Palestinian,' the main leader of the Ain el-Helweh jihadist network."

Ain el-Helweh is the largest Palestinian camp in Lebanon—home to seventy-five thousand people in a square mile of squalor that still lacks clean running water fifty years after its establishment. Ain el-Helweh is the headquarters for a more established jihadi organization, Asbat al Ansar, another Sunni terrorist group affiliated with Al Qaeda. Operatives from Asbat al Ansar had assassinated five Lebanese judges two years earlier. They were connected to terrorist bombings of the Russian embassy and fast-food restaurants in Beirut.

Traveling into Ain el-Helweh was a risk even with the proper permissions from the Lebanese army colonel who stamped my official document, a step that ensured only that he knew my name and passport details if I didn't come back. Lebanese government authority ends at the last army checkpoint before the camp entrance. Ain el-Helweh long had been a safe house for the region's radicals, including a fugitive from the 1993 World Trade Center bombing in New York. It had harbored every Palestinian militant group but now Islamist groups inside the camp had grown in influence because of an infusion of foreign fighters from Iraq. Officially, Fatah, the nationalist Palestinian faction, was in charge of the camp. Fatah also was responsible for my safety. Heavily armed Fatah men squeezed me into the middle seat of a dusty Mercedes for the short ride to headquarters. As we drove, I had to consider that I had entrusted my well-being to five scruffy men wearing faded military uniforms and plastic sandals. They were on edge. So was I.

The narrow streets of the camp were empty. A shoot-out with the Lebanese army the night before had raised fears that the confrontation with Fatah al Islam in the north would spread. Many of the residents, mostly women and children, had fled the camp and were allowed to shelter in public parks in Sidon. The jihadists stayed behind, indoors and out of sight. We drove through deserted streets lined with concrete apartment blocks connected by low-hung electric and phone cables that formed a wire web overhead. On every wall were posters of the political trends represented here: Fatah, Hamas, Palestinian Islamic Jihad, Asbat al Ansar. Saddam Hussein, a Sunni Muslim, was still a hero for some here and rated a poster on the grey walls.

I was ushered into an office and introduced to General Mohammed Ali Abeet, who said he was the Fatah commander. He had two cellphones on the desk and paused often to take urgent calls. The general appeared to be in his sixties. His military uniform was spotless and pressed, his boots clean and polished. Mohammed Ali Abeet projected dignity and authority in this small grimy office. But the younger men around him, who had pressed into the office to listen in on our conversation, were dressed in mismatched uniforms and plastic footwear. This ragtag group was the sad picture of a movement in decline.

In between phone calls Mohammed Ali told me that he had been negotiating with the men of Asbat al Ansar to calm the tensions in the camp. "We have a very good relationship. We work together in order to contain what's been happening. We make efforts to keep the situation under control." But it was clear that Fatah was the weaker partner in the relationship. In time this secular Palestinian nationalist movement likely would lose out to the more powerful ideology of worldwide jihad, just as secular Pan-Arabism had lost out across the region following the collapse of Iraq. For young Palestinians, the bearded disciplined jihadist militants—men of action, professional fighters who had returned from Iraq—could make a stronger appeal for their loyalty and offer an escape from the frustration of the long and failing struggle for a Palestinian homeland.

Ain el-Helweh had been built in 1948 for refugees from northern Palestine, Arabs who had to make way for the new Jewish state. Fatah's commander, Mohammed Ali, had probably grown up in the camp, risen through the ranks of Fatah, and fought in Fatah's military campaigns. An older man now, he knew his and Fatah's time was coming to an end. He wanted me to understand that he still believed in his lifelong nationalist struggle but he was up against the reality of the dismal life inside the confines of this place. He was losing the battle of ideas to an ideology that was based on anger and revenge. Jihad promised paradise in the next life, which seemed a better deal than the failed promises of Fatah in this life. "In order to have such groups, three things must be present," he said, explaining how Asbat al Ansar had gained a following in his camp. "Poverty, ignorance, and loss of hope, and these are present in many of our communities. These young men have no way out. They have no jobs. They have no future." He was deliberately giving me a message in a bottle to take out of the camp, from which Mohammed Ali himself would likely never leave. He would, like Palestinians of his generation, be born to, and live largely within, a "temporary" refuge for a people denied a home. His life had not escaped the camp. He knew that younger men, looking at his experience, would not tolerate it for themselves. Fifty years of frustrated hope were enough.

Bernard Rougier had analyzed Fatah al Islam in the context of what he knew about fundamentalist groups in Lebanon. For more than a decade he had kept contacts with the Palestinians in Ain el-Helweh and Lebanon's militant Sunni Islamists in Tripoli. He had documented their embrace of global jihad. The war in Iraq had sped up a clock already ticking in Lebanon. Sunnis. Shiites. The divide was already here. In 2006, Hezbollah, then part of a coalition government in Lebanon, went to war with Israel. The decision was taken without consultation. A Shiite militia had become the most visible force in Lebanon. Just as they were in Iraq, Sunnis in Lebanon were on the defensive, marginalized and bitter.

Many Sunni extremists accused Hezbollah of making southern Lebanon an exclusively Shiite zone, effectively keeping them away from the Israeli border. Sunni Islamists accused Hezbollah of forcing

them out of the fight with Israel and so Lebanon became their bat-
tleground instead. "For them, it doesn't matter if you do this here or
in Iraq," said Rougier. "So, these are the winds of regionalization and
it is very strong. No one is trying to impede those winds blowing
into this country. And this is why it is a serious situation in
Lebanon. . . . Lebanon is also another place to fight the Americans,
and the West."

There were many symbols of the West in Beirut and across the
country. We were sitting in a traditional Beirut café, surrounded by
waiters carrying trays of Arabic coffee, with plates of salty almonds
and olives on the table. The Starbucks across the street was more
popular, crowded with well-dressed Lebanese who now preferred the
simpler American version of the afternoon coffee ritual. The McDonald's hamburger chain had opened in every district in the capital, and
the outlet in the Bekaa Valley was packed with Hezbollah supporters
ordering Big Macs and supersized sodas. Children crawled over a gar-
ish Ronald McDonald statue in the restaurant's outdoor grassy play-
ground. It was possible to stop in at Dunkin' Donuts shops from
Beirut to the Syrian border. Another Western symbol, the blue hats
of the United Nations peacekeeping force—composed of French,
Spanish, and Italian soldiers—patrolled southern Lebanon as part of
a larger international force. In Lebanon, there were many "Western"
targets.

The newcomer had arrived in 2006. The Palestinians of the Nahr
al Bared refugee camp noted these recent refugees, distinguished by
long beards and assault rifles. The new men kept to themselves and
didn't smile much or talk to women; when they did speak it was to
admonish camp residents for playing music, smoking, posting pictures,
and other perceived sins against religion.

One aspect of Lebanese politics that security chief Major General
Ashraf Rifi had skipped over in his explanations of the country's cur-

rent problems was how Lebanese factions and outside groups had deliberately used the Palestinians to advance their own sectarian or political interests. Most Lebanese are unaware, or choose not to be aware, of the abject living conditions for the 400,000 Palestinians who reside inside the confines of the camps. The Palestinians were barred from holding jobs or otherwise engaging in the national life of Lebanon, even though many had never lived anywhere else. Ghassan Moukheiber, a member of Lebanon's Parliament, summed up government policy: "Our official policy is to maintain Palestinians in a vulnerable precarious situation to diminish prospects for their naturalization or permanent settlement." The Lebanese government considered the refugee camps a security problem rather than a social problem. In fact, they were both, and worsening.

In the northern camp, the war on the militants was sparked when Fatah al Islam employed one of its fund-raising techniques: a bank robbery. The bank job went wrong from the start. Lebanon's Internal Security Forces trailed the thieves back to an apartment block in an affluent Tripoli neighborhood, which turned out to be a militant safe house. The security teams stormed the building at dawn. When news of the fight reached the nearby camp, Fatah al Islam militants attacked Lebanese army units, slaughtering more than a dozen soldiers. The army struck back with great force. The fight lasted more than ninety days.

"A religious and cultural problem" was Rifi's diagnosis. "We are putting on the brakes. We asked religious people to step in." He suggested I meet an imam who was working with the jailed militants of Fatah al Islam. Lebanon had adopted a campaign modeled on a successful project developed by Saudi Arabia and Yemen to deal with returning jihadists. They had to be reprogrammed. But Rifi hardly seemed confident that it would work: "You can't expect a fighter to come back and open a vegetable stand. They need rehabilitation. You must change them from being a fighter to being a civilian. These men have seen blood, they've seen power, and they've seen death."

So did Lebanon have an extensive rehabilitation program to deal with the battle-hardened radicals? "Unfortunately, no. And this is the second time we are making the mistake. When they went to Afghanistan and they finished their missions there, no one cared for them. So we paid a heavy price. This is the second time. Iraq. No one has started to prepare."

The Lebanese government declared victory over Fatah al Islam in September 2007, and so this mini-war was finally over, despite the escape of Shakir Absi, Fatah al Islam's leader. He had been declared dead more than once, and a body finally presented to the media as Absi's corpse failed a DNA test. Absi had disappeared, but reemerged over the following months vowing revenge through mysterious audio recordings. Roadside bombs exacted that revenge against the Lebanese army, but the primary victims of the conflict had been the Palestinians living in the Nahr al Bared camp on the outskirts of Tripoli. They had been forced out of their homes by the battles, and months passed before they were allowed to return to the camp. Even then, only a few thousand were permitted to live in the partially damaged buildings of a neighborhood on the outskirts of Nahr al Bared.

I finally reached the camp, after weeks of negotiations, with a Lebanese army escort. We passed through multiple army checkpoints on a blindingly sunny day. Mohammed Yusuf, a Special Forces officer who had a role in the battle, was the guide for a drive through the battlefield. The dirt roads that had separated neighborhoods had been cleared but buildings were empty shells, pancaked piles of concrete. The internal walls were blackened and burned; bullet holes marked every partially standing structure.

"It started here, on Hamra Street," said Yusuf from the front seat of the car as he directed the driver past piles of concrete. No signpost marked this particular place or distinguished this dusty path from any other in camp. But Yusuf knew it was once a main avenue that led out of the camp, to where the Lebanese army was stationed. "This is where they hit the Lebanese soldiers the first time. When they killed them. At the top of this road. It was always a military checkpoint."

The battle began when the militants inside the camp had surprised the Lebanese army, some asleep in the hours before a shift change. In a pre-dawn attack, they had crept up on the soldiers and slit more than a dozen throats. The barbaric act had galvanized Lebanese public opinion and sparked a desire for revenge among members of the Lebanese army, most of whom were locals from the north of the country.

Yusuf, from the north himself, was still seething about those deaths, angry about the four-decade-old rules that prevented the Lebanese army from entering the camps. The restrictions were imposed when Palestinian nationalist organizations were strong enough to enforce law and order inside the camps, but times had changed and Yusuf reflected the Lebanese army's feeling of impotence. "If we had been able to come in then, we might have been able to put a stop to it," he bitterly complained.

I asked Yusuf if the lessons from what happened in the camp had been learned in Tripoli.

"The Palestinians have learned the lesson here in Nahr el Bared. But on the outside of this camp, in the other Palestinian camps? No. They still have this ideology in their heads," he told me. He was convinced that this was a Palestinian problem. They had welcomed the militants. They were to blame. They had to pay a steep price.

"Before the war, they made a million dollars a day. Income! In one day," said Yusuf forcefully, an acknowledgment that the Palestinians had been integrated into the Lebanese economy, especially here in a vast market that attracted Lebanese customers from Tripoli as well as from the capital, Beirut. In the last leg of the drive out of Nahr el Bared, we passed a short row of vegetable and fruit shops that had opened again. Once a much longer line of shops had sustained the major produce market for Lebanese and Palestinian families. Until the battle with Fatah al Islam destroyed almost everything.

"The Lebanese came from all over for the low prices. Everyone came here to shop. They lost it all," said Yusuf, reflecting a widespread opinion among Lebanese, especially in the north, that the Palestinians were now unwanted, rejected because they were the carriers of a radical ideology that could destroy Lebanon.

"I am not scared to tell the truth. Most of the Lebanese authorities know what happened," said Mohammed, a Palestinian who was nevertheless afraid to tell his full name because he worked for a Palestinian charity. His "truth" could cause more harm. We met in his office outside the camp after my official tour of Nahr al Bared. Mohammed had a home on the outskirts of the camp. After an education in Sweden, he had come home to work for a Palestinian educational institution. He had lived in Nahr al Bared for six years. He had evacuated in the first few days of the fighting, left everything behind, to escape the shelling and the gunfire. When the battle was over, he expected the Lebanese army to allow the residents to return. But the wait continued. Nahr el Bared was sealed shut by the Lebanese army. Mohammed knew a soldier, a man he considered a friend. He asked for help.

"He agreed to check on my apartment. He asked me 'what do you want?' Only photos. Only that. Everything else I can buy with money. But I can never take those pictures again. Of my children. He brought me the pictures. I was lucky."

More than six weeks later, when the Lebanese army opened the camp for the first time, Mohammed and other returning Palestinians were heckled by checkpoint soldiers and Lebanese demonstrators who had come to shout abuse. Every house had been destroyed; much of the destruction had come after the fight with Fatah al Islam was over.

"I saw by my [own] eyes that the Lebanese soldiers burned the houses. In my house, there was nothing left at all. Not a chair. Not a paper. Nothing at all." Fire had gutted every room.

"The fire was not a normal fire. I could see a fluid on the walls. That is how they started the fire. Maybe diesel fuel, by the color. In the kitchen, and in the bathroom. I had nothing to be burned. So why was it so black? You can notice that something had been spilled." The Lebanese army had systematically destroyed the infrastructure of the camp, in an attempt to make it impossible for the Palestinians to return. Mohammed had documented the demolition. He opened a computer to a file full of photographs. The digital case file was collected and downloaded by Palestinians who had slipped, unnoticed, into the camps.

I could see pictures of Lebanese soldiers, in uniform, struggling under the heavy load of a refrigerator they had dragged out of an empty house. Everything left behind by the camp residents when they fled the battle—gold, cash, photo albums, documents—had vanished. Cars parked on the streets were crushed, run over by bulldozers.

As Mohammed clicked through the photo gallery on his computer, I also saw images of men in black masks—the men of Fatah al Islam, training for battle soon after they arrived. Mohammed has also documented the rise (and fall) of the newcomers. "They had a lot of money," Mohammed told me. "They could buy anything. They had weapons with night scopes, this is very expensive. How could they get these weapons?" In time, there was a military training camp, even a military parade, on the main street of the camp.

"They were polite and kind but that is not enough. They were criminals," Mohammed said about the men who had caused so much havoc. "What made me so frustrated, most of them were from Saudi Arabia, from Syria, from other Arab countries, only four or five of them were Palestinians. The Lebanese criticized us because they say we helped them and we cooperated. Why don't they criticize Saudi Arabia for sending them? They never say that the Saudis are bad."

Mohammed shuffled through the pictures once more to make sure I saw the entire gallery. It was a private collection, representing a documentary account by the camp residents. There was no point in sharing the information with Lebanese authorities, Mohammed told me, because he believed they would do nothing about it. As the head of a Palestinian charity, he was aware of the damage to his already weakened community, including stepped-up medical visits for ailments rooted in depression and despair.

"How could two hundred outsiders enter Nahr al Bared?" he asked, demanding an explanation for how Fatah al Islam had gained access. "They came legally through the airport. And Lebanon's Internal Security Forces had to know."

Mohammed kept his eyes on the images of the bearded men with guns. He was not immune from the despair that had engulfed his neighbors and friends. He had enough influence to save old personal photographs, but not enough to save his home. He would have to rebuild again.

"Look, maybe the Lebanese were after a victory, like all Arab armies; they haven't been in victory, so, just to show that they are strong. But they were fighting against the walls, against the stones, against these empty houses. I don't think they needed to destroy six thousand houses to kill two hundred terrorists. Fatah al Islam was a fly on their head. When they tried to kill the fly, they brought a hammer. When the fly escaped, they hit themselves on the head."

A few days later in Beirut, I arrived for an appointment at Musjid Thee al Morayen, the Mosque of Two Lights—a historical reference to Islam's third caliph after the death of the Prophet Muhammad. The name signals that it is a Sunni mosque. The Musjid Thee al Morayen and the imams here are part of Lebanon's Sunni mainstream establishment.

Inside, Imam Osama Shehab looked like an old-time sage, with a long white beard, a soft white robe, and an embroidered prayer cap on his thinning hair. He smiled broadly when I walked in, welcomed my interest in his work. A flat-screen television was tuned to the news in one corner of his office, the sound turned low. Shehab explained that he had learned about human nature from his long years working in Lebanon's prisons. He was the official imam who worked on death row. For fifteen years, he had prayed with men, comforted them, before they went to the gallows.

His current assignment was to the Special Wing in Lebanon's central jail, the terrorism section of the main prison. The rounded-up, arrested survivors of Fatah al Islam were the latest inmates. He understood that his assignment was the new approach to fighting radicalism in the country. He was the reprogrammer. He had preached against flawed interpretations of the Koran. He had urged moderation at his Friday sermons in Beirut. For years he had preached against those who interpreted the Koran as advocating violent jihad. Now he was bringing his message to a hard-core audience behind bars. His job was to counsel, discuss, and, over time, hopefully convince the prisoners that their interpretations were wrong. Despite being part of the government's Sunni religious establishment, he had gained some trust, maybe even some converts.

"Some of them didn't know they were coming to Lebanon," he told me in describing the inmates from Fatah al Islam. "They said they were brought from Syria, not across the regular borders, but across the mountains. Some of them claimed that they were fighting against Israel. They came for the purpose of fighting Israel and then found themselves fighting against the Lebanese army without knowing it."

Why had these men from Fatah al Islam come?

"You feel that some of them have a sense of oppression. They observed that there is a global and international attack on Islam. So, this extremism against Islam created in them an extremism to defend Islam," said Shehab. And, surprisingly, he added that he too felt it. The imam charged with reprogramming the jihadis sympathized with the motivation that had led the Sunnis to take up extreme violence.

"Let us talk openly," he began. "To practice Islam in Lebanon, a country that is open and secular, we, as Muslims, feel that there is an ongoing war against Islam here." Shehab, a deeply religious man, was in conflict with his own culture, Beirut's secular, materialistic society. Perhaps that internal conflict was the reason he related to the prisoners. He understood the reasons for their rage. "Islam tells us to preserve the family. I have teenaged daughters. They walk in the street and they see nude pictures. I want to preserve my family and I am afraid for the morality of my children."

Lebanon's advertising culture was on display just a few blocks from the mosque. On large billboards, sex was in the service of selling everything from the latest jeans fashion to soft drinks and furniture. Western culture had seeped into almost every aspect of life surrounding the mosque.

"One time a drunken man entered our mosque, and another time, a drunk was running naked outside the mosque after he got in a fight. I feel these things are directed against me, against my religion, because there is no respect for my religion and my rights," the imam said. An educated, spiritual man, he wanted me to understand his distress, the pressure of living a religious life in a secular culture. He was fifty-five years old and the modern world was bearing down on his soul.

I nodded my head and he appreciated the gesture. I had heard this line of complaint often enough in my own country. Shehab was a gentle, moderate man overwhelmed by forces he could not control or change. He wished to live his life as a good Muslim, a man of simple faith—an objective not easily met in the sectarian mix of his Beirut neighborhood. He understood the emotions that drove other men to take up arms, but he vehemently disagreed with their methods. His greatest challenge was to convince men who had fought in the name of religion to shed the convictions that led to violence but to retain the convictions that, in his view, led them to God. He understood their dilemma.

Perhaps the greatest test of the imam's beliefs and his identity as a religious leader, as a Sunni Muslim in a country where the power-sharing included Shiites and Christians, was an undeniable fact about the terrorist wing of the prison. All of the inmates were Sunnis. Only Sunnis. No Shiites or Christians had been arrested under Lebanon's terrorism laws.

"Why only Sunnis?" Shehab's question was insistent and angry. "Is this because of some outside pressure? Is it because the fighters in Chechnya, in Kashmir, and in Iraq, these movements are Sunni?"

No Shiite prisoners in the terrorist wing? I asked again to be certain I understood his answer, that there was not a single Shiite or Christian jailed there.

Again, it was the Sunni-Shiite divide. For Osama Shehab, the Sunnis were under the threat of Shiite domination in Lebanon—as he believed they were in Iraq. The Arab order, Sunni dominance in the region, was under siege. Even to this moderate cleric, it was evidence of a wider transformation in Lebanon and in the region—another legacy of the war in Iraq.

CHAPTER EIGHT

"EVERY IRAQI CITIZEN IS A LANDMINE ABOUT TO BLOW UP"

The Iraqi woman in the white head scarf had tears in her eyes as she made her appeal to the uniformed Jordanian policeman. "Please," she said desperately, sliding her passport closer to his hand while reaching out to touch the shoulder of her young daughter to indicate that the plea is not just for her but for a family in danger.

The young officer's face was impossible to read. He consulted another guard, more to delay the final encounter than for any reprieve. Then, with a slight shrug, he returned her passport without the purple entrance stamp. The woman and her daughter would have to return to Iraq.

A twenty-five-year-old Iraqi dentist named Mohammed posted the details of harsher treatment in Jordan on his blog "Last of Iraqis."

> Then an officer came to us and told us that we aren't going to enter
> Amman in the most humiliating way of speaking, and walked away.
> I tried to talk to him but he closed the door in my face. I was so
> angry of the way he treated us, we are locked in a small room now,
> and my wife is scared of closed places, she began to cry hysterically
> I felt that she will die if she staid [sic] like this and again there was
> nothing I can do.

Jordan began shutting down the border in 2005, when three coordinated hotel bombings killed fifty-nine people and brought the Iraq
war to Amman's doorstep. The suicide bomb teams were connected
to the Sunni Islamist militant Abu Musab al-Zarqawi. While protes-
tors in Amman chanted "Burn in hell, Abu Musab al-Zarqawi," they
were also convinced that Jordan, known as the gateway for Westerners
into Baghdad, was targeted for Jordan's close alliance with the United
States. The suicide bombers had arrived in the tide of Iraqi refugees
crossing the border.

Soon after, Iraqi men between the ages of seventeen and forty were
barred entry. Unofficially, the country was already closed to Shiite
Iraqis even before the bombings. Jordan made no secret of its dread
of Shiite rule in Baghdad. King Abdullah was the first Sunni Arab
ruler to publicly warn of a dangerous "Shiite crescent" of power spread-
ing from Tehran to Arab lands. Jordan keenly felt the end of Saddam's
long rule as the downfall of the Sunni power structure. Jordan had
ties of commerce with Iraq and blood ties to Iraq's Sunni Arab tribes
with branches that crossed national borders. Before the American invasion, it was well known in Washington that the Hashemite kingdom
had been a key to Saddam's financial survival. Jordan facilitated illegal
oil sales that generated billions of dollars in unmonitored revenue, un-
dermining the UN sanctions in place since 1991. After the invasion,
Saddam's daughters were allowed to quietly settle in the Jordanian

capital. Senior Iraqi military officers bought up expansive villas and stayed out of sight. Jordan had long served as a haven for Iraqis. Shutting the border was an unusual step.

Jordan had been wide open between 1990 and 2003, the only refuge available for Iraqis after the first Gulf war in 1991. Over time, the more than one million refugees, including Egyptian and Palestinian workers, returned home or moved on to Europe and the United States. More than two hundred thousand were granted political asylum and resettled elsewhere. By 2002, the remaining Iraqis had settled permanently in Jordan, mostly in the capital, Amman.

The exiles who began to arrive in the spring of 2003, few in number at first, were among the Sunni Muslim elite, Baath party members who had become prosperous under Saddam Hussein's rule. These wealthy businessmen came to buy apartments and install their families in Jordan's quiet capital until American intentions were clear. They could easily afford the rigorous Jordanian requirements for legal residence in the Hashemite Kingdom. Seventy-five thousand dollars deposited in a Jordanian bank bought a legal residence along with comfort and safety.

As the population of wealthy Iraqi exiles grew and the cash flowed in with them, parts of Jordan prospered. The cranes and jackhammers signaled a building boom in Amman, and property prices doubled almost overnight. Taxicab drivers found plenty of new customers who were unfamiliar with Jordan's confusing road system. But the exodus continued as thousands of poorer Iraqis arrived at the border without the means to buy a long-term legal stay.

Jordan's policy for legal residency in the Kingdom created a two-tier system. The poorer exiles, barred from working and on overextended visas, could barely survive and lived in fear of deportation by Jordanian police who rigorously checked Iraqi passports for invalid visas that included a per-day per-person fine of about $3 for staying past the legal date. The international humanitarian organizations that set up shop in the Jordanian capital publicized the refugee crisis and lobbied for millions in aid, especially for Jordan's education system. But many Iraqis kept their children out of the school system, believing that Jordanian authorities could track them down through enrollment records. Even the sign-up at the United Nations High Commissioner for Refugees office was a dangerous exercise. Iraqis applying for refugee status could be hauled off the line in security sweeps and whisked away to jail, or worse, to the airport, where they were given one-way tickets to Baghdad.

However, there was an older generation of Iraqi exiles who had formed a community in Amman. They lived quietly and safely; some had jobs in universities or in the private hospitals in the capital. They were businessmen, journalists, artists, poets, and educated profession-als who met over Iraqi kabobs and milky glasses of *arak* in the new restaurants opening all over town specializing in Iraqi cuisine. They had quietly celebrated the fall of Saddam; some had gone back to see their homeland, but their dreams of a permanent return to Iraq were on hold.

"Everybody dreams of going back. It was a dream and it was totally against the grain of reality," said Jawad al-Assady, an Iraqi author and playwright. One of his plays was on the program in a well-attended Arabic Theater Festival at Jordan's King Hussein Cultural Center. Al-Assady, elegant in his cream-colored tailored suit, with long white hair and dark skin, had been outside Iraq for more than twenty years. An established author, he shuttled between Paris and Rome, taught the-ater courses in Damascus, opened his own theater in Beirut, and served as a consultant for culture ministries in the Persian Gulf. His was a typical résumé for an accomplished Iraqi émigré. In Amman, he could count on a large Iraqi audience for his work. His plays were about the Iraqi experience, the yearning of a generation for a lost homeland and the aching experience of exile. European audiences had read and applauded his work, but he was convinced that only an Iraqi audience would truly understand him.

"For those who did dream, that dream is now dead for the generation in their fifties and sixties. This is what causes so much pain to me. I cannot go back," lamented al-Assady. I suggested that times might change. Surely he could reconcile with the new Iraqi state? Perhaps in a few years he could reconsider?

"For me, it is impossible to live in Iraq. I wanted to see my people, my friends. I had big dreams to take my theater there. I tested the situation and after that I decided. It is impossible because they will kill you. It is impossible to live there with this kind of mentality and this kind of life."

In April 2003, the day that American soldiers had pulled Saddam's statue down in Firdus Square in Baghdad, al-Assady had watched the unfolding drama on television from a hotel room in Abu Dhabi. "I cried. I couldn't believe you could get rid of him. It was like a huge weight lifted off my chest," he told me as he swayed slightly, eyes closed. The physical memory of that day remained part of the telling.

Al-Assady made plans to go back, and then put off the departure. "It would have been better if I had gone right away," he told me. "But then, when I saw the looting and the way things were going, it made me think again. And I always said wait. After that, I decided to go back because I wanted to see my house and my relatives, my city." Al-Assady arrived in Baghdad at the end of 2004, when the signs of civil war were already apparent. He met with theater people, staged a play, and surveyed the city at a dangerous time. He had kept in touch with relatives over the years. He knew it would be bad; he had heard them describe the ravages of the regime. But now, to see Baghdad for himself, the squalor, the resentments, he could not reconcile his memories with the facts on the ground.

"I couldn't believe how much Baghdad had changed! It was as if Saddam had taken this beautiful city, a city of light, and just burned it and put in its place different buildings and different homes. He had scarred and disfigured Baghdad." Iraq, the rich and beautiful country of his youth, was now a Third World place. And the people, the Iraqi people, he went on: "Maybe you noticed how a person becomes a beast from the inside, and the outside becomes frightening. This was a different city and a different people. These were no longer the people I knew. This was not my memory."

It was a measure of Saddam's totalitarian state that the exiles, even those who kept the closest contacts, had not fully understood the vast changes his despotic regime had wrought. They remembered a secular, cosmopolitan country, nights on the Tigris with open bars, the free-wheeling oil-rich days before the years of Saddam's wars and the long, punishing United Nations sanctions that had impoverished the population in psychological as well as material ways. But their memories were just that: memories.

After Jawad al-Assady left Baghdad, he mulled the experience and shaped it into a play. *Years Elapsed Without You* was his meditation, an indictment really, on the Iraqi character, a dramatization of the moral decay, the barbarism, the empty shell he believed Iraqis had become. "In this play, I announced my loss of hope. Not in the Iraqi person, but in the Iraqi society. I think it is difficult to think Iraqis will ever go back to what they were."

The play is set in 2004, in wartime Baghdad. The stage directions call for a constant clatter of gunfire, helicopters, and explosions. The characters inhabit an old house, chandeliers in the hallway, a stack of books, a television, a sofa at center stage. The story dramatizes a reunion, a device that creates family tension and portrays the divide between those who left and those who stayed. The son and his new wife return from London after twenty-three years abroad. They remark on the change in the nature of the people, observing that "inside every Iraqi citizen is a landmine about to blow up at you any second."

As the drama progresses, the family reveals that the father, a former Marxist philosophy professor turned looter, had amassed vast real estate holdings based on cash stolen from Iraqi banks. His accomplice, a brother who had served as a torturer during Saddam's regime, must hide in the house or face retribution from revenge-seeking neighbors. The daughter, who has retreated into her room and religion, was unhinged by a kidnap and rape. Al-Assady's portrayal is darkly comic, a tragic vision of a damaged society beyond repair or redemption. In his drama he has rendered a soulless land while his own dreams of return lie in ruins.

Saba had lived the Iraqi nightmare that playwright Assady portrayed. Saba and her family lived on a quiet side street on the outskirts of Amman. My Jordanian taxi driver had to search for the exact place, slowly circling streets that looked similar, until Saba's father finally guided him by cellphone to the specific apartment block. The neighborhoods of white-stone-block and tinted-glass apartments had sprung up quickly during the cash-fueled boom driven by the first wave of Iraqi exiles. Saba and her family were there legally, but not permanently.

Saba's father was waiting on the curbside when I arrived, and greeted me warmly. He looked like the former Iraqi military officer that he was: trim, erect, with the standard-issue mustache. This was our first face-to-face meeting, but we had formed a bond over his family's tragedy. We had met online, by chance, two strangers, one in Baghdad and the other in Damascus, both with the same goal: to help nineteen-year-old Saba after she had been shot in the back.

I had done nothing more than forward his plea for help to a friend, Jamie Tarabey, who worked in the Baghdad bureau for National Public Radio. She had performed the miracle, reaching contacts at the U.S. combat support hospital known as the CSH (pronounced "cash") calling in whatever capital she had in a city with an overwhelming number of people who needed miracles to survive. Jamie had phoned, persuaded people, and worked through the night to help a young girl she didn't know, a stranger, who was dying in a Baghdad hospital. Others sent the same imploring messages, from Washington, from Amman, and had called in favors. Saba's survival was due, in part, to an e-mail alarm that had rocketed around the globe. But it began in Baghdad. Her father's e-mail message was short, direct, and grave: "The bullet entered Saba's chest and exited through her spine. She is bleeding internally and can't feel her hands or legs. She desperately needs medical attention."

Saba's father, reflecting his military training, had included necessary details about his daughter, from her blood type to her location on a trauma ward. Baghdad was full of cases of anonymous suffering. But this victim had a name and a father who was reaching out to save her life: She had a chance. Hope dies last, as Studs Terkel rightly pointed out.

By dawn the next morning, my e-mail inbox showed a fresh message from Lieutenant Colonel Gunther Hsue, a doctor on duty at the military hospital in Baghdad. He was the self-appointed contact for anyone who had been part of the long e-mail chain of rescuers. "We will do everything in our power to see if we can get Saba triaged at the CSH. This is subject to multiple layers of scrutiny due to the political/administrative shifts of personnel of the CSH (new staff changeover just weeks ago) so I don't exactly know their policy or rules of engagement on these kind of cases. However, I have contacted a prominent clinical staff member who will represent Saba's case and at least consult with the Ortho/Spine surgeon."

A few minutes after I read the e-mail, my phone rang in Damascus. On the other end of a crackling line from Baghdad, Lieutenant Colonel Hsue assured me that Saba had been transferred to the 86th CSH Ibn Sina hospital inside the Green Zone. She was in the operating room, he said, shouting into the receiver. He wanted me to know that all of the military surgeons on duty that night were women and they had taken a keen interest in the case of a nineteen-year-old Iraqi girl with a gunshot wound in her spine. Saba was doing fine, he yelled, and he would call with an update on her case.

Gunther Hsue sent more harrowing medical details by the end of the day. "Saba is recovering from surgery. Per the ICU staff, she has at least paralysis from the mid-back down right now. They are looking into options to get her out of the country (somewhere in the Middle East) so she can rehabilitate—preferably in a center specializing in spinal injuries."

This time he had included a picture with the latest update. Dark-haired Saba looked straight into the camera, her expression a mixture of anger, grief, aggression, and pain. A nineteen-year-old Iraqi girl in a wheelchair doesn't have many options in Iraq. This much was clear from the grim face staring out from the photograph. Saba had survived the long surgery. She was getting the best care possible at the U.S. military hospital in Baghdad. She would live, but she might never walk again. And there was nothing more that could be done in Baghdad. Iraq's healthcare system, once the best in the Middle East, had collapsed. Anything beyond emergency care was beyond its capabilities. Saba and her family were going to Amman, Jordan, for further recovery.

Propped on a bed of pillows in Amman, Saba looked much younger than her nineteen years. She was dressed in powder-puff pink pajamas, her thin, still legs barely filling out the fabric. The bedroom, where Saba spent most days and nights, had a magical theme.

Disney princesses in pastel ball gowns smiled down from posters covering the walls. A Minnie Mouse watch ticked off her long hours of inactivity. Bottles of glitter nail polish decorated the mirrored dressing table. The closet wall was a clutter of photographs from Saba's stay at the U.S. military hospital. She shared the bed with more than a dozen oversized stuffed animals, gifts from the U.S. military surgeons who had saved her life.

Saba's mother served a tray of milky coffee and cookies, as the family gathered around Saba's bed. Her care was now the family focus. Sarah, twelve years old, and Mustapha, twenty-two, spoke the clearest English in the family, but Saba's father struggled to articulate the one thought, the overwhelming guilt, that played through his mind every time he remembered the day that Saba was critically injured. He felt he had failed his daughter, failed to keep her safe.

"I am a security officer," he said grimly, shaking his head at the memory of that day in Baghdad. "I made sure the driver had a security plan for driving Saba to the university. I sent my son out of the country to keep him safe. She is a small girl. Just a small girl! I could not imagine that anyone would want to shoot a small girl."

Saba's father had survived four years of upheaval in Baghdad by being careful and learning to adapt. Early on, the Americans had dismissed him from his army job, along with all the Iraqi officers he knew, and he had suffered in those months without an income. But soon he'd been hired as a security chief for an American aid agency—Western women had come to Baghdad to help Iraqi women. He had kept his job secret from his neighbors and most of his family and had kept to himself his pride that no one on his watch had been injured or killed.

He had trained as a security officer in the military and understood that the American women who came to Baghdad to teach equal opportunity and equality in Iraq's conservative and increasingly religious society would need his skills. He even came to believe in their mission. After all, he had two daughters, Saba and Sarah. Saba had the strongest will of his children and he had supported her when she enrolled in Baghdad University to study computer science.

As Baghdad became more dangerous, he assessed the threats and decided to send his son, Mustapha, to Syria with enough money to live on his own for a while, in the spring of 2007, thinking he would be able to return home soon. The American military had a new strategy for Baghdad, a new security plan to protect civilians. The family lived in Yarmouk, a mixed neighborhood, with a majority of Sunnis, and many of his neighbors were former military men. In the summer of 2007, neighborhood outposts known as joint security stations opened in Yarmouk. Former Iraqi military officers, Sunnis, walked the streets with the Americans.

For Saba's father, this was a new and promising trend, as was the emergence of pro-American leanings among the Sunnis in Anbar province, the violence-prone region west of Baghdad. The risk of targeted sectarian killings in Baghdad still loomed; his son had been threatened, but Yarmouk was more stable than other neighborhoods and the family stayed close to home.

"I was threatened personally," explained Mustapha. At Baghdad University in March 2007, the one place he went outside his neighborhood, "the head of security on campus saw me and drew his hand across his neck, and he whispered, 'I am going to kill you.'"

Mustapha told his father that the head of security was also a member of the Jaysh al-Mahdi (the Shiite militia known as the JAM), and Mustapha and his father agreed that the threat had to be taken seriously. But once Mustapha was safe in Syria, the rest of the family, including the two sisters, stayed on in Baghdad until June, the end of the school year. The family plan was to join Mustapha in Syria for the summer and return home as soon as they all thought the security prospects had improved. Saba, though, was restless almost as soon as she arrived in Syria. She had loved her time at university. If the family remained outside of Iraq for long, let alone permanently joined the mass of Iraqi exiles, she was sure she would miss the chance of a college degree.

All through the summer of 2007, Saba watched news reports aired by Iraqi state television and trolled news sites online at the Internet cafés in Syria. She always brought the most positive stories about Iraq to her father's attention. For Saba, Syria—crowded with hopeless Iraqi exiles having nothing to do and running out of money—was a dead end. She begged her father to allow her to return to Baghdad when classes began again in the fall.

Her most convincing argument came unexpectedly in November 2007, when Prime Minister Nouri al-Maliki made his $800 appeal to Iraqi exiles to come home. Saba had watched the announcement on Iraqi television, and she was touched by the emotional public service announcements that ran nonstop, showing happy returnees.

"Between Iraqi families, there was always a desire to go back," she said, defending her reasons for pressing her family to return. "People told us it was safe. We knew a lot of people who were thinking of going back."

I asked if they had considered signing up for the government-sponsored bus.

"We took a bus, but not the government bus," said Saba. To get back to Baghdad in time for the first week of university registration, the family agreed to go a week earlier than the government-sponsored trip. However, Saba failed to convince Mustapha to join in the return to Baghdad. He decided to stay behind in Syria for a little longer. The rest of the family arrived home on November 21, at a time when the intense heat of Baghdad begins to taper off soon after dark and the nights are cool enough to sleep indoors rather than on the roof.

The first two weeks back home were pleasant and uneventful. The family enjoyed the improvements in the neighborhood since their trip to Damascus. The electric power was now on up to twelve hours a day and new volunteers, Sunnis, were patrolling some neighborhoods in

Baghdad. It was possible to believe that Iraq was finally stepping back from the abyss. In Yarmouk, at least, the sectarian feud that had cost so many lives had abated. The American surge of soldiers had brought some stability to the capital and General David Petreaus had cautiously said, "We are close to a sustainable level of violence."

Saba registered at the university for her second year in computer science. Her father hired a man he trusted, a friend he knew from his military service, to drive her to the campus each morning. He drilled the driver on the best security practices and routes, then recruited two other neighborhood families whose daughters also wanted a safe ride to school.

"At 7:30 in the morning, the driver of the mini-bus came by the house," he recalled. "She got in and then went to pick up her friend in the same neighborhood. After five minutes we got the call from Saba, 'I've been shot.'" Without even thinking, she had dialed her father on a cellphone moments after a bullet pierced her spine.

Saba vividly recalled the attack: "I saw the blood all over me. When he shot me, I couldn't feel my body. I thought I was dead. But how could I still use the phone? So, I knew I was still alive. My friend's father thought I would die."

The mini-bus driver had arrived a few minutes early at Saba's doorstep because one of the girls, preparing for a family wedding, decided to skip class that day. The third passenger was a few blocks away, and when the driver pulled up to the curb he cut the engine.

"The third girl was always late. So we knew we would have to wait," Saba told me. Her father might have insisted that this was a breach of security, had he known of the habitual pattern. As Saba and the driver waited in the morning quiet, she saw a young man step up to the driver's window. Dressed in a crisp white shirt and grey trousers and carrying a heavy book bag over his shoulder, he looked like a university student. He told the driver he wanted a ride to another college and wanted to leave at once. The mini-bus driver, annoyed by the interruption, said, no, he didn't drive to that college. "But I am in a hurry," the young man insisted. Saba remembered his impatience. She remembered he had an ordinary face.

"All of a sudden, he took out a pistol and shot the driver four times, very calmly, like he was prepared," said Saba, remembering the details from the film that replayed in her head.

"After the driver said, 'I'm sorry,' the young man just shot him. Four shots. And then he started to look at me in a weird way. Then he shot me. He didn't have a car. While he was running he started shooting at the mini-bus. I heard the bullets passing around my head. After he ran, I looked out and I saw that he had stuffed his gun in his book bag. By that time, I was only half-awake."

There was no one else on the street, Saba recalled. The gunshots may have brought residents to their windows to watch as a young man, a student, in a white shirt and grey trousers, galloped down the block, a heavy book bag thumping against his shoulders. But Iraqis had learned from hard experience to stay behind closed doors when shots are fired. The family inside the house directly in front of the mini-bus kept its doors closed, too.

"I started to shout like hell," Saba told me. "The third girl's father was afraid to come out. Then he thought I was going to die. So he brought me into the house. And I called my father again. After ten minutes, my mother and father arrived."

The shooting in the Yarmouk neighborhood was an event that happened in the "weeds" as the military jargon would have it, deep down, on the street level. Saba's story showed that Baghdad still roiled with revenge and deadly militias, still seethed with mistrust of American intentions and distrust between Iraqi neighbors.

Saba's parents arrived quickly at the scene of the shooting after their daughter's call for help. She was critically wounded and needed immediate emergency care, but taking her to a hospital was an uneasy decision for Saba's family. They knew that the neighborhood hospital was controlled by the Jaysh al-Mahdi. Mahdi militiamen guarded the hospital entrance. Saba's mother recalled that they knew a neighbor who worked at the hospital and hoped that he could negotiate their wounded daughter's way into the emergency room.

"Because, if you are from the north, you are Sunni, and those in the hospitals are JAM. So someone had to help us get past the guards, otherwise they would have completed the job." Saba's mother, an Iraqi with a distinctive accent from her birthplace of Mosul who carried a Sunni identity card, could still not walk unprotected into a Baghdad hospital without fear of retribution from the Shiite guards.

"An army officer offered to help us. He was also a Sunni." This was the first lucky break, the result of the new political reality coursing through the Sunni community. Sunnis, who had once opted out of participation in the new Iraqi state, were now on patrol in some neighborhoods. Even in her weakened state, Saba knew that the army officer could get them past the militiamen at the hospital's front door.

"So now, we had three people helping us. The army guy was responsible for the area; he was with us and accompanied all of us to the hospital. Not only him, there was a military unit who came with us. Dad was an officer and they came to help us so we would survive it."

But the hospital was not equipped to deal with Saba's traumatic wounds, recalled Saba's father. "The doctors said we were in a hard situation. They wanted money. They saw the wound and advised us to take her to another hospital in Baghdad that might be better able to help her. She had internal bleeding. She died twice in those first couple of hours. The doctor at that point said to us, 'Wait for two days, she will probably die. I am sorry.'"

Saba felt that she *was* dying. She could feel the weight of the blood pooling in her body. She had enough strength left to make a personal appeal directly to the doctor. Her parents were surprised that she still had the power, in a strong, clear voice, to shout from the emergency ward gurney, "I am so heavy, I am filling with blood! Help me!" She collapsed from the exertion of the effort. But the doctor was unmoved and unequipped. He only repeated his prognosis to her frantic parents: "Wait for two days, she will probably die."

Those were the words that sent Saba's father out of the hospital and into the night to find a working Internet line where he could convey the details of his daughter's wounds, the events of the day, and the Iraqi doctor's prognosis. He begged for help. He hit "Send" and waited. He could not get back into the hospital without the help of the Iraqi military officers who had gotten him past the guards. There was nothing else for him to do but wait.

When the Humvee pulled up to the emergency entrance to the Baghdad hospital, he knew a miracle was possible. The rescue team had his cellphone number; they knew his daughter was a patient at this Baghdad hospital. They were Americans, they were armed, and they were transferring Saba to the Green Zone, to Ibn Sina hospital. He knew this place. The facility had been a military hospital for officers in Saddam's time. Now, it was staffed with an American medical team with plenty of experience in treating gunshot wounds.

"After two hours they got her into surgery, otherwise she would have died," said Saba's father, who waited outside the operating room. She stayed at the ICU for five days. The Americans called her "the girl who wanted to survive."

The women military surgeons on duty were told that Saba's father had worked as the head of security for an American aid organization. They knew that he had protected a group that helped Iraqi women. They worked hard that night to save his daughter, and Saba got extra attention in her recovery because "the girl who wanted to survive" had charmed the medical staff.

As Saba recounted her days in intensive care, her mother handed me a plastic folder containing the medical records of her daughter's injuries. She pointed to the one English word she had come to understand, "paraplegia," in the medical description that showed "t-3/4 injury with canal intrusion." The records included Saba's first psychological assessments after surgery, the interviews with a counselor when Saba had learned that she might not walk again: "She has an intact sense of self, sees herself as intelligent and friendly. When asked directly if she would have desired to live if she were to find out that she would remain paralyzed, she became tearful and said no."

The picture that Lieutenant Colonel Gunther Hsue had sent me by e-mail was taken at about this time. Saba's father continued the story because the next few days were as harrowing for him as the actual shooting. As his daughter struggled to recover from an operation to remove a bullet from her spine, he returned home to care for his younger daughter and faced the surprising reaction of his neighbors.

"The rumors in the neighborhood started almost right away," he recalled. "The neighbors would say, 'Oh, you work with the Americans.' They started to say that Saba and her mother must have worked as translators. That is the only explanation for their acceptance into the American hospital." They were not pleased with Saba's survival but, rather, took it as a sign that a family secret had finally been revealed.

This was a hazard Saba's father hadn't considered when he reached out for help. He had always kept his work with an American aid agency a secret. The connection had helped save his daughter's life, but now his suspicious neighbors were convinced that his wife and daughter were the traitors. Never mind that neither Saba nor her mother spoke English, or that some of his neighbors had signed on to work with the Americans in the joint security stations in the neighborhood. Saba's admission to an American military hospital was the damning proof that the family had long-term connections to the Americans. He knew that this kind of talk was dangerous. It would bring his final break with Iraq.

"I started hearing these bad words from the neighbors. They would say, 'Your daughter should be dead, but you work with the Americans.' That's when I knew we had to leave. Maybe I would survive in Baghdad, but Saba, emotionally, she can't." In the hospital recovery room, Saba would cry every time she heard a gunshot. She started to see gunmen in her dreams.

Saba had been in the hospital for five days when the medical staff reevaluated her progress and concluded that she was well enough to go home. She was stable, and there were others in line for her spot in the intensive care unit. But where, if Yarmouk was no longer safe? Saba's father was convinced that bringing his daughter home would incite retributions. "I said this is impossible. They will kill her again." But she wasn't well enough to travel yet and a medical evacuation, in her fragile condition, from Baghdad to Amman was pricey: $10,000, out of reach for the family. How long before she would be well enough to travel on a commercial flight? He had no idea, but he asked the hospital to delay Saba's departure for as long as he thought he could get.

"I asked Ibn Sina for three more days. They gave us those three days. I booked a first-class flight. We told the Jordanians this was a medical emergency and they had an ambulance waiting." Saba's father had resisted the pull of exile for four years. He had always been convinced that Baghdad was not just his home but his future. Now, there was nothing left to keep him there.

Saba made the final leg of her journey in the first-class cabin, bracing against the corkscrew takeoff that protected pilot and passengers from rocket attacks from the ground. Saba's father rented an apartment in the Jordanian suburbs known as Little Baghdad. He hired a physical therapist and an English tutor for his daughter. He understood his daughter well enough to know that she needed to keep her mind as well as her body active. On the day I visited the family in Amman, Saba showed flashes of the spirit that had won her a following among the military doctors at the American military hospital in Baghdad. But time was not on her side. With each passing week, her legs atrophied, her paralysis weighed on her mind.

On the bedroom table, there was a brochure from an American medical institute in Atlanta, Georgia, that specialized in treating spinal injuries. The glossy pages showed a facility that looked like an American resort, with patients walking on the grassy grounds. With a promise of "advanced technology in rehabilitation" the center specialized in a device that stimulated lifeless legs. The family had applied to the American embassy in Amman for a medical visa. Saba's father knew every detail of the specialized device. He had plotted out the finances and contacted relatives in America who agreed to support the family until Saba could walk again. This, he believed, might be the solution to the nightmare that had almost crushed his family.

"All the respectable people have left, the rest are criminals," he said of his Baghdad neighbors as he repeated his own mental journey in convincing himself and his family that they must quit Baghdad for good.

He moved his family to Jordan for an eighteen-month stay. It took that long to get the call from the International Organization for Migration (IOM) directing them to Atlanta, Georgia. Saba and her family would now be near the rehabilitation facility that advertised a specialty in resuscitating lifeless limbs; at least that is what Saba believed when she sent me an e-mail in the winter of 2008:

> *Merry Christmas and happy new year, I hope you're doing well*
> *I wont to told you that we're at last going to the US, we depart Amman airport in 28th January 2009 with IOM program, to new york city then to Atlanta Georgia the city which we want to live in and start my treatment there.*
> *best regards*
> *Saba*

Saba's success highlighted the failure of Iraqi refugees who were rejected for U.S. resettlement. These Iraqis presented Jordan with long-term challenges. Jordan had been weakened after the fall of Saddam and the fracturing of the regional Sunni alliance. But Jordan remained a Sunni refuge for Iraq's Baathist army generals, air force pilots, intelligence operatives, and business elites who had crossed the border early for an indeterminate stay.

CHAPTER NINE

LOST GENERATION

Nezar Hussein never wanted to become a refugee. He refused to register at the United Nations refugee office in Damascus. Prematurely bald and unnaturally mature for his twenty-seven years, he wore a pendant of the map of Iraq under his shirt, a talisman against abandoning his homeland. "It's not about being a patriot. I am asking, what do I want to do with my life?" Many Iraqi exiles in Damascus shared his contempt for the refugee designation; only about 10 percent of the population had filled out the UN paperwork. Nezar's plan was to eventually return to Baghdad. In the meantime, life in Damascus was a constant struggle, his creativity, he lamented, dimmed by the enforced idleness.

Nezar, a charming wise-ass, was my guide to the exile community of young Iraqi artists in Syria. Artists were under threat in Iraq. Again. Under Saddam, art had been debased to serve as propaganda. Indeed, almost all the public art in Baghdad portrayed an image of Hussein or a reference to his Baath party. Iraq's long tradition of poetry and letters was a particular danger to the regime, and many artists had been jailed or forced out. Now, a younger generation of artists was jeopardized by the new intolerant ideologies dominating the country. Iraq's cultural heritage was under siege. The statue of Abu Jafar al-Mansur, the Abbasid caliph who founded and built Baghdad during the eighth century, had been toppled along with a stone memorial to the Baath party—the work, it was said, of Shiite militants who saw offense in this particular artistic heritage.

For the most part Nazar was guarded about his feelings, focusing instead on translating from Iraqi Arabic into English to help me convey the tragedy of others. But when he was in a reflective mood, Baghdad was often on his mind.

"We saw a whole city being destroyed, looted and burned, but our reaction? It wasn't enough. I mean, people have choices." Nazar's hands were in the air, accentuating his indictment against his friends, his family—Iraqis—whom he believed had failed to stop Iraq's transformation into something unrecognizable.

Nazar recalled the day American soldiers arrived in his Baghdad neighborhood during the spring of 2003. "First of all, when I saw the Americans, it was a double feeling. I am happy and I am not. My question at the time, what would happen later?"

He recalled his first English sentence spoken aloud. "Rebuilding this city will be easy, rebuilding its soul—that will be difficult" was his statement to a Western news crew that had stopped him in the street. Like many Iraqis of his generation, Nezar had learned English by listening to bootlegged music tapes and American movies. His first English sentence spoken in public contained a profound observation. He had described the immense but unacknowledged task of the U.S. project in Iraq, rebuilding a fractured society traumatized by Saddam Hussein and his regime. "It was a line from a movie that I remembered," he admitted sheepishly.

Nezar had believed the U.S. invasion would free him from Saddam's mental prison. His deep desire was for personal freedom. Democracy was fine if that's what Iraqis wanted, but as far as he could tell the first set of policies put in place by the Americans who came to govern Iraq were ominous. "They made this ruling council, and every month we had a new president. Wow. We have nine presidents, one every month. What the fuck is this? We have one for thirty-five years, and then one every month. Okay, guys, we are hungry for changing our president, but not like this."

While a university student, Nezar was part of an underground artist's movement known as Jama't Najeen, the "Survivors' Group." A loose collective of Iraqi filmmakers, actors, painters, and performers, the "Survivors" came together after the first Gulf war in 1991. Most of them had attended the Institute for Fine Arts in Baghdad. For a decade, the group organized shows in private homes and student apartments to avoid censure by Hussein's Ministry of Culture. One "Survivor" was expelled from college for refusing to make a sculpture of Saddam Hussein for his senior project.

With the arrival of the Americans, the goal of the "Survivors"— personal and intellectual freedom—became tangible. They believed they could build a "new" Iraq through art and the revival of Iraq's "true" culture. In the chaotic days after the fall of Saddam, members of the "Survivors' Group" organized quickly and moved into the Al Rashid Theater in Baghdad as the city was overrun by looters who were plundering or burning the remnants of the Iraqi state. The Al Rashid is Baghdad's most famous playhouse, a national treasure, a venue that was open for the first time to these dissident artists despite gaping holes in its roof and still-smoking rubble.

"When I was sitting inside the theater, I wanted to show that the Iraqis were not just about looting," Nezar explained. The "Survivors" were taking a stand against the chaos enveloping Baghdad, committed to protecting the Al Rashid from further damage with a twenty-four-hour-a-day vigil. It was a symbolic act, an attempt to claim and protect part of their cultural heritage come what may.

They celebrated the successful theater protection campaign by writing and producing a play called *They Passed by Here*, which premiered on May 4, 2003. The accompanying music was the Beatles'"Nowhere Man," an apt description for young Iraqis in their twenties and early thirties who considered themselves part of a "lost generation," cut off from the rest of the world, left out of globalization because of Saddam and a decade of United Nations sanctions. They were toddlers when the Iran-Iraq war began, adolescents when Saddam invaded Kuwait, teenagers in the 1990s during the disastrous years of privations following the UN sanctions, and young adults by the time the Americans arrived.

This "lost generation" was the majority in Iraq. At the time of the U.S. invasion, nearly half of the county's citizens were under twenty-one years of age. Unlike Nezar, many of his peers had decided to join the Shiite militias, the Sunni insurgency, or Al Qaeda in Mesopotamia, including some of his friends from his university days.

At the Al Rashid Theater in Baghdad, fueled by cigarettes, *arak*, and all-night sessions, the "Survivors' Group" hatched a plan to produce Iraq's first post-war feature film. The writing began in 2003—and the film became a real possibility when the group located a twenty-one-year-old Ariflex camera at a theater-and-television production company in Baghdad. The next break came when hundreds of rolls of 35-millimeter Kodak film showed up at Baghdad's silver market, in canisters looted from the Ministry of Culture. The "Survivors" borrowed money to buy up every roll. The film stock was clearly marked with the official government stamp and a 1973 purchase date. Following an e-mail appeal, a Kodak company official agreed to help them, writing back that to shoot on outdated film was the act of a fool or a genius. The Iraqi cinematographer, Ziad Turkey, explained simply: "You may question why we're shooting on old negative film with an old-fashioned camera, but the answer is that we have nothing else."

The film was titled *Underexposure*, in a wry acknowledgment of the outcome of shooting a film on old Kodak stock, more than sixteen years out of date. The crew had a pledge from Kodak to mix up a special soup of chemicals in Kodak's motion picture laboratory in Beirut. When the first experimental batch was run through the process, the lab crew sent a message: "Underexpose the film while shooting." It was a risk, but also a canny bet. The story of the group's determination to jump-start Iraq with the tools at hand was a great marketing ploy. In 2004, the film production group got backing from the German government. Another message went out to Lebanese composer Gabriel Yared to score the film. Yared's acceptance, with his list of movie music credits, including *Cold Mountain* and *The English Patient*, convinced the "Survivors" that the clock had finally started again on movie making in Iraq. "I am an Arab, a Muslim, and I lived under Saddam," said the film's director in interviews at the time. "Those are reasons enough to be imprisoned for over thirty years. We are still blinking incredulously at the sun."

The sun showed even brighter during the film's 2005 premier in worldwide film festivals and at awards ceremonies, a triumph for the "Survivors' Group." Some of the cast and crew traveled out of Baghdad for screenings in the Czech Republic, Japan, Singapore, the Netherlands, South Africa, Germany, India, and Spain. The release of *Underexposure* was accompanied by glowing reviews that seemed an antidote to the growing despair that was engulfing Baghdad. "Iraq's first uncensored feature in over a decade!" was the excited headline on an Australian website ahead of the showing. "A cast of characters riddled with both hopelessness and promise—a determined filmmaker working with only expired film, an eloquent poet weak with cancer, a wounded soldier wrapped in bandages and prayers but on the brink of death, an old man full of memories of Baghdad that are now only nostalgia, and most importantly, a city in rubble still filled with desire, compassion and perseverance." In this film within a film, the narrative revolves around a filmmaker who documents the life of his friends and neighbors throughout the American invasion and the aftermath. The film highlights the destruction of Baghdad with haunting shots of a city in ruins. The old film stock did not register the vivid greens and the reds of the Iraqi capital; the film colors are dusty and subdued as if reflecting the early reactions to an American occupation. The grimy, yellowed scenes of the city also reflect a time window that was closing, a brief era of possibilities that was slipping out of reach.

By the time *Underexposure* premiered in Baghdad, in the violent spring of 2006, the era of possibilities had expired. The civil war was under way. Death threats arrived soon after the film was shown. The first target was the young Iraqi actor Samar Qahtan, who had played the lead role. The offense, explained Nezar: "He was drinking in the film, and he was cursing the war and the militias. Only that. He was drinking and he cursed, and there is a scene where he is half-naked with his wife. She is also half-naked and he is touching her leg and kissing her." Who complained, I asked. "Islamic people, I don't know." Nezar looked away for a moment, anticipating the next question.

"This was 2006. Didn't you know that this was going to happen?" I asked. He took his time before answering. "Yeah, yeah," he finally said. "It was not a secret."

"What we did was very selfish, produce a film. What did we change?" said Nezar, shaking his head. "We shot the film over twenty months. The city was falling apart, the militias were coming. We saw it all. We had the sense this was our last chance."

"All of us are liars. Everyone knew what would happen when we showed the movie in Baghdad." Nezar stressed this point so I would not misunderstand. He had taken his name off the official credits. "It is always your decision what you want to do. If you are thinking of flying away, if you decide you want asylum you will do things to make it happen. You will do things."

His revelation that the film crew had anticipated the death threats—that they actively sought a documented reason to leave Iraq—didn't surprise me. Saddam had been a master at teaching generations of Iraqis a survival instinct that involved a measure of deception and sometimes self-deception, honed for so long that most Iraqis engaged in it without thinking. The filmmakers had called themselves the "Survivors," and they meant to be just that. It turned out that their yearning for personal freedom wasn't attached to a particular country. Iraq was in ruins, the timetable for rebuilding was uncertain, so they had made preparations for a future somewhere else. They had witnessed Iraq's descent into violent madness, had incorporated the wounds into the narrative of the film, and then used the film to move on.

Underexposure was a resettlement ticket. A documented death threat could be useful. Iraqis had been fleeing the country for three decades; almost every prominent family had a relative who had to get out. The documents needed as qualification for resettlement were well known. A credible death threat was important proof that remaining in Iraq was not viable.

But Nezar Hussein had not settled on exile. He believed that if he accepted resettlement, turning his back on Baghdad, then he could no longer be an artist. Torn between two worlds, he wasn't fully at home in Damascus, even though he was surrounded by many "Survivors" who had left Baghdad but intended to move farther away.

The director of *Underexposure* had been granted asylum in Germany after an invitation to work there from the German officials who had helped fund the film. Another member of the crew applied for a scholarship to the UCLA film school in an online competition and, remarkably, won a place in Los Angeles. The director of photography had moved his wife and children to the town of Zabadoni, outside of Damascus, and signed up for resettlement with the United Nations. So far, only one member of the "Survivors' Group" had returned to Baghdad. Five days after his arrival he was killed in a car accident outside of Baghdad. No one was certain whether he had been targeted or his death was an ironic misfortune. Either way, the death was an unsettling warning that the time was not yet right for return.

In Damascus, Nezar was struggling to accept that everything he had loved about Iraq was gone. Iraq was a different country. Even a peace in Iraq could not change that truth. He acknowledged that the old Baghdad had not been an easy place. He'd had some close calls. As a student at the Fine Arts College during Saddam's time he had been dragged out of a lecture room, arrested, and tortured for three weeks at Abu Ghraib prison. He was hung by his shoulders and beaten, he told me, and his joints still cracked when he lifted his arms. At the time, his friends were convinced he would never return. "It was a case of mistaken identity," he explained, which is why he survived. He had spent three weeks in bed recovering from the ordeal. But there were parts of his old life that he prized—his family, his friends, the familiar streets and neighborhoods of Baghdad. He was sure of his identity. He was an Iraqi. But where was his Iraq?

Nezar Hussein's friends in Damascus were obsessed with finding a way out of the Middle East. Legal resettlement to the United States was an option for only a very few. Iraqis were desperately searching for other routes out—but no country wanted to take them in. "I'm sure you know about this, it's not a surprise for anybody reading newspapers," Nezar had written to me a few weeks before my return to Damascus.

He wanted me to meet two young dancers, friends of his, also members of the "Survivors' Group" who were waiting for visas to Holland.

Muhanad Rasheed, the lead dancer, apologized for his tattoo after he swept his dark hair off his face and saw me looking at the black letters on the side of his palm. Thin and fine-featured, Rasheed was dressed in loose gym pants, a T-shirt, and a leather jacket. The black letters read "Life Is Bullshit."

"How long have you had that tattoo?" I asked.

"I was seventeen. When I made it, this was my reaction to life. It was a mistake, and one day I will delete it."

After a pause, he added: "Life is not bullshit. My thoughts are changing. You should respect life, and it was a reaction then. We should live life and do our dreams."

Rasheed, a Sunni from a prominent Baghdad family, had honed his dream down to one simple goal—get out of Iraq, get out of the Middle East. He shoved both hands into his pockets against the cold of the day and the memory of the time when he had carefully inked the indelibly bleak assessment during what would turn out to be the last years of Saddam's rule. A swell of music, two lingering piano notes, interrupted our conversation, as sound engineers tested the theater acoustics for Rasheed's modern dance performance later in the evening. This was his cue to join two other male dancers for warm-up exercises on the cold stage. The Teatro in Damascus, outside the walls of the Old City, was a converted Damascene villa, built around a stone courtyard that smelled of citrus from the tall bitter-orange trees growing along the grey walls.

Tonight, the stage was reserved for Rasheed's dance troupe, "Iraqi Bodies," and the Iraqi stage crew was checking the sound system and the lighting and strategically placing large space heaters near the rows of white plastic chairs to counter the winter chill that lingered in the stone floor and walls.

Rasheed was wary of divulging personal details apart from why he was in Damascus. Like the tattoo, those details were part of a past life that he had closed off and packed away. When I asked why he had left Baghdad, he simply said, "Life is more important than art. I didn't want to die there."

He told me he was a choreographer. He said he had joined Iraq's first contemporary dance company in Baghdad in 2003, a few months after the Americans arrived. He had gotten interested in Japanese folk dance when an Iraqi who had immigrated to Sweden in the 1990s came back home in those first months after liberation and held workshops on contemporary dance. This was Rasheed's first experience of globalization and it had changed the direction of his life.

He had joined the "Survivors' Group" in college. His older brother, Oday Rasheed, had been the writer and director of *Underexposure*. Rasheed had his own credit on the film, as the clapper loader and sound engineer. But dance was his passion. He and the other Iraqi men in the troupe, one of them his younger brother, planned to claim political asylum in Holland. They hoped to become citizens of the West: artists, individuals, turning their backs on Iraq, probably forever.

"We got an invitation to go to Holland, dancing in a festival that will take place in Amsterdam and then in Rotterdam. Now, we are working in Damascus, but I can't see a future here." He was uncomfortable talking about the future in more detail. His focus was on the present, the rehearsal for the evening performance as his friends prepared the theater space.

Rasheed had worked hard for an invitation to a European dance festival. Creating a coherent dance meant he had to shrug off the emotional numbness that was the state that most Iraqis preferred. His life revolved around long rehearsals and frequent performances in the hope of attracting the Western embassy crowd. He had met a Dutch dancer in Damascus and she had arranged the invitation to a festival in Amsterdam. The theme was "Dancing on the Edge"—a week of performances and debates on contemporary dance in the Middle East.

Rasheed had waited in nervous apprehension for the visa from the Dutch embassy, hoping that he had convinced suspicious officials that his plan was to go to the festival and return to Iraq even though he had no intention of going back.

For him, the end of Saddam's regime had stirred an unquenchable, individualist yearning. So how could he go back to a society increasingly based on tribal values and sectarianism? He tried to express these emotions in a ninety-minute dance that he called "Crying of My Mother."

"It is about three men, all brothers, and we find there is a problem between them. They are fighting. But they don't know why they are fighting each other. What is the reason? We don't know. And then we find that one of them kills the other one." Rasheed outlined the ideas he was trying to convey in simple and controlled movements on the stage that combined a Japanese art form with Iraqi folk dancing.

"I want to say that we are the main problem. It is a flaw in our culture. We can look to history, but the main problem is us. Iraqis. I am trying to describe the problem, the problem of our culture. Why do we try to kill each other? I know a lot of Iraqis don't agree with me, but this is what I want to tell."

To Rasheed, most of what had happened since the U.S. invasion of Iraq was a self-inflicted wound. Americans were to blame, but so were Iraqis who embraced violence as a way to negotiate daily life.

"There are a lot of Iraqis who have this problem. Even I have this problem, and that's why we kill each other. I understand there is the American military in Iraq, but we are the ones who have to fix the problem."

Rasheed had raised all the questions that I had been asking since my first trip to Baghdad after the American invasion. What kind of country will Iraq become? How can Iraqis forgive the unforgivable violence that they inflicted on one another? How could they erase the Sunni-Shiite divide? What is the future for this fractured, suspicious society emerging from decades of Saddam's rule?

Muhanad Rasheed—like Nezar Hussein, one of the lost generation—had grown up during the harshest years of Saddam's regime, a lifetime of almost constant war and privations. Now, Rasheed had created an artist's rendering of one of the central dilemmas for his homeland. He believed it would take years to rebuild an educated middle class necessary to modernize the country, now that the mostly Sunni middle class had fled. The individualism that was at the core of the American version of democracy was likely out of reach for the generation growing up in the new Iraq.

Rasheed's personal answer to the questions he had posed might be considered selfish. Iraq needed him back to help rebuild the country. He wanted to start a new life, despite the uncertainty of exile and the risk that his creative days would be sapped by the rigors of an exile's life. But he was still young. He had time to adapt to a new culture, learn a new language. Art—and, in particular, dance—was turning out to be a successful tool.

The Dutch visas finally came through a few days before the performance, adding extra emotional energy to Rasheed's farewell. The audience at the Teatro was mostly Syrian but also included staff members from the cultural departments of Western embassies and a few Iraqis beyond the circle of friends of the dance troupe. Rasheed and his brother, Duraid Abbas, basked in the standing ovation as lights faded to black along with the music. Muhanad Rasheed had produced a dance about deadly brothers and performed his critique of Iraq with his own brother at his side. They would go to Holland together. They would be survivors.

After the final show, a small group of friends gathered for a more personal farewell. Nezar Hussein, after videotaping the last dance, had organized the party and he guided the group through the cobblestone streets of the Christian quarter inside the walled Old City at the heart of Damascus. He settled everyone in a nearly empty bar with a surprisingly good sound system and a remarkable library of American rap tunes where we danced for hours, fueled by cold Syrian beer and American cigarettes.

A few nights later, in Nezar Hussein's one-room basement apartment, Rasheed and his brother Duraid made final preparations before their plane was scheduled to leave. I watched them sort through their belongings, packing small suitcases for the next phase of their life. They used up their last cellphone minutes saying good-bye to family in Baghdad and in exile in Damascus. Nezar was not celebrating the departure even as he helped the brothers pack.

"I love my friends very much, all of them. I consider them family and part of me, and I am happy that they are able to travel, apply for asylum, and get passports. But my heart really aches when I think that they won't be with me."

A few days later, another group of Iraqis arrived after a fourteen-hour bus ride from Baghdad before leaving for Europe that night. This group had invitations to a film festival in Milan, Italy, and all of them planned to apply for asylum once the festival was over.

In a corner of the small airless basement apartment, five young Iraqi men were sitting cross-legged, trading stories and sharing photographed memories that they had saved on white laptop Mac computers. They laughed over their Italian visas, handwritten in their passports because the printer in the Baghdad government office had been broken, but convincing enough for the Syrian border officials. They listened to sad ballads on computer speakers and lingered over family photographs and mourned young friends who had been killed. These "Survivors" were determined to start again someplace else.

These young Iraqis had signed up for the "Information Age," which promised individual choice and a borderless world. They wanted to be part of the global grid, off-limits in Saddam's Iraq. The pressing problem for these ardent twenty-something soon-to-be exiles was what to buy in Damascus for a new life in Europe? A Che Guevara baseball cap was the most common purchase to augment a simple wardrobe. They still considered themselves revolutionaries.

Nezar Hussein watched over his flock in this way-station of the Underground Railroad out of the Middle East. "We thought we would revitalize film in the Middle East; now, we're just refugees, wasting time," he reflected. But they had been lucky. Art was a ticket out.

Nezar, however, could not imagine a future for himself in Europe. "They stay there for five years, taking new papers, getting a passport, changing nationality. They are taking a benefit, they are being selfish. They are not taking responsibility. I am not saying, 'Go to Baghdad and die. No. Be smart, just be smart.' I am saying, 'Go and be smart.' I love them really, I do. But I mean, they did their choice, but my choice is something else." With every new departure, Nezar sank noticeably further into gloom—a particular paralysis that many exiles say is the hardest part of leaving home. He didn't want to be just another émigré in Europe out of touch with Iraq, but he couldn't find a way home either.

Young, talented Iraqis could count on the hypocrisy of an official European refugee policy that had closed the door on large-scale resettlement. Unofficially, Europe cherry-picked the cream of the crop of asylum seekers. The larger exile community turned to illegal immigration— a tide that rose in 2007, when Iraqis tried to get out of the Middle East by any means necessary.

Iraqi exiles gambled with their lives by hiring human traffickers rather than risk the promise of improved security in the Iraqi capital. The cost of tickets onboard the illegal underground route was a testament to the hidden resources of the exile community. Traffickers charged up to $15,000 per person for a "first-class" journey by air to Europe with forged passports and real visas. A more precarious option— climbing inside the tank of a truck to share the dark space with twenty other men, women, and children—could cost $1,500. Everyone knew someone who had made it. The routes were well known, posted on websites, the successes and failures discussed and dissected.

Malaysia and Indonesia still granted visas to Iraqis, and those countries became the gateway to Australia. The overland road through Turkey was the most-traveled way out. Iraqis started this journey by boarding small inflatable boats, which took them across the Aegean Sea to the Greek islands near the Turkish coast. In 2007, asylum applications in Greece rose by 205 percent. Another route was via a ferry line that Syria had recently opened from its coastal town of Latakya to the port on the Turkish portion of Cyprus. The ferry link had been an expression of a new era of political friendship between Syria and Turkey. In the summer, Syrian tourists crowded on board for the holidays. But by the winter of 2007, the passengers were mostly Iraqis who had no intention of making a return trip.

When I visited the Turkish attaché in his office in Latakya, he was surprisingly frank and told me that the ferry was now a smugglers' boat. "Why else would anyone take the trip in the winter?" he said as we both rubbed our chilled hands near the office heater. He explained that winter gales and rough seas would often delay the trip for days; even so, the ferry was booked for weeks. One young man I met told me that traffickers charged $5,000 for the trip, which would end just short of the Cyprus coast. The Iraqis then swam ashore in the freezing water with their documents and dry clothing wrapped tightly in a plastic sack. Smugglers would transfer them from the Turkish side of the island to the Greek side of Cyprus, which they believed was their first step to asylum in the European Union.

Of course, there were horror stories about con jobs and Iraqis who died in meat lockers on the Turkish highways. Some disappeared without a trace, or reappeared in Baghdad broke, disheartened yet committed to raising the money to try again. Others got trapped in Nigeria or Cambodia without documents and did jail time before they were deported. Still others were busted on a passport line when they didn't have a plausible story to explain why they couldn't speak the language of the country in which their passport claimed they were born.

But there were enough success stories to register a 10 percent rise in the asylum statistics for the European Union in 2007. The army of Iraqi illegal migrants, more than fifty thousand strong, was determined not to go back to Baghdad. By 2009, exhausting every legal delay, some Iraqis had been rounded up by immigration authorities for forced repatriations, but for the most part they survived in adopted homes in Europe.

Rasheed's and Duraid's asylum applications were accepted by the Dutch authorities and filed within weeks of sold-out dance performances in Amsterdam and Rotterdam. The two brothers were fast-tracked for resettlement and assigned an apartment in a community of refugees. They were eligible for a stipend that provided for living expenses. They were free to pursue the careers of their dreams. If they regretted leaving Iraq they didn't say so when they called Nezar Hussein in Damascus. Indeed, they were in high spirits marveling over Amsterdam's quaint cobblestone streets and their good fortune. Nezar shared their joy, shouting into the phone that he missed them. The "Survivors' Group" had finally quit Iraq.

The dance "Crying of My Mother" was a hit on the art circuit in Holland, Greece, Lebanon, and Iran. These young Iraqi artists had diagnosed the country's deepest psychosis but could offer no solutions aside from dancing out of the cauldron. "My sense of identity during war is not an issue, because then I am totally Iraqi," explained twenty-four-year-old Rasheed, in an interview at the start of a European tour in 2009. "When I left, I realized I don't feel a sense of 'place' anymore."

CHAPTER TEN

"BEHIND EVERY DISH LIES A WORLD, A CULTURE, A HISTORY"

Why are Iraqis so obsessed with Iraqi cuisine, I asked Mohammed Yahya, an Iraqi refugee himself, as we waited for our dinner in a restaurant popular with the exile community. "Because it is so delicious," Mohammed said. It was an answer without irony that implied I had asked an absurd question. Iraqis loved their meat-centric cuisine that seemed, to my untutored palate, variations of lamb, fat, rice, onions, and tomatoes. However, I also observed that the longer Iraqis were in exile, as they realized that home was on hold, the more they focused on Iraqi fare. For Yahya, and many of the exiles, Iraqi cuisine was like football, an expression of patriotism—part nostalgia and part identity, a symbol of Baghdad's distinct character. "When Syrians taste our food, they know it is better, too," Mohammed said as a way of expanding his explanation. But there were no Syrians in the room. The dinner customers surrounding us all spoke with a distinctive Iraqi accent.

In the short space of a few years, the Iraqi exile neighborhoods in Damascus had been transformed into faithful recreations of Baghdad. The Syrian streets took on names that reflected Iraqi cities and sects. *Shaku Maku* was the preferred greeting, an Iraqi slang that served for "Wassup, dude," blunter than the genteel colloquial Arabic of Syria. More than thirty Baghdad restaurants opened Damascus branches with established names that featured particular Iraqi dishes. *Pacha. Masgoof. Quzi. Guss.* The restaurants and cafés were an archipelago of undiluted Iraqi culture in the Syrian capital. In these establishments, Iraqi chefs prepared dishes using special Iraqi spices, Iraqi beans, and Iraqi rice—and, most important, they served fresh, hot *samoon*, the distinctive soft-crusted, chewy bread that had become comfort food for the Iraqi exile community.

Zarzoor, in Damascus, was crowded most nights, with waiting lines out into the street during Ramadan. The original Iraqi *Zarzoor*, on the main highway in Fallujah, was considered the best kebob joint in the country, well worth the hour-long drive from Baghdad, until it was wiped out by the Marines in the battle of 2004—considered a national calamity until the succulent kabobs were available again, though far from home. The Iraqi master chefs in Damascus who roasted fish for authentic Iraqi *masgoof* had insisted on importing river fish from Baghdad until they came to believe that the taste was tainted by dead bodies in the Tigris River. Afterward, *masgoof* restaurants featured farmed carp from the Syrian markets instead. No one complained.

Damascus did not lack fine cuisine of its own. Syrians were rightly proud of their culinary heritage. A new class of capitalists, liberated by the easing of Syria's socialist economy under Bashar al-Assad, opened world-class restaurants that offered the delicate cuisines reflecting Syria's rich history. Renowned European food writers offered dining tours of Damascus, and avid travelers sampled the delights of the city's most famous kitchens. The aromatic dishes of Aleppo, the pistachio- and pine-nut-laden kabobs available in Syria's northern city, influenced by its historic role as a capital along the Silk Road trading route, and by its location at the tip of the fertile crescent, had earned awards from the International Academy of Gastronomy in Paris. The preference for Iraqi dishes among the exile community wasn't even a question of price. Food was a relatively cheap commodity in Syria, a cornerstone of a domestic economic policy that subsidized bread and fuel. For Iraqis, food was a matter of memory and national pride.

In legend and in fact, Baghdad claimed a celebrated role in defining Arab cuisine. Recipes were written down more than a thousand years ago when Baghdad was the richest city in the world, with dishes named after connoisseur caliphs of the Abbasid court who defined a golden age of cooking. The Abbasids ruled over a diverse population that contributed to the variety of cooking styles, spices, and ingredients, influenced as well by the more sophisticated palates of the conquered Persians. Historians have written that vegetable dishes were introduced to the court menu by the caliph's physicians, mostly Nestorian Christians, who were convinced of the health benefits. The pre-Islamic diet of dates, barley, and dairy was revolutionized by an urban empire that prized good food and memorialized fine dining in the poetry of the court. Complex stews were the dish of choice, a fitting metaphor for a land that accommodated so many differences.

In modern times, Baghdad had a thriving food culture from the bounty of the fertile agricultural land watered by the Tigris and Euphrates rivers. When I first came to Baghdad more than two decades ago, during the height of Saddam's rule in the early years of the Iran-Iraq war, the gentle curves of the Tigris River were lined with *masgoof* fish restaurants, lush parks, and nightclubs, open late into the night for a population that considered the complexly herbed succulent roasted fish a national treasure. In this oppressed society, where Western journalists were always under the watchful eye of a "minder" from the Ministry of Information, an evening spent on Abu Nawas street was a welcome release as well as a place to relax and spend a few hours in Iraqi society without the presence of a government official.

Iraq's diverse population had defined culture and cuisine, but it was also the cause of some of the country's greatest tragedies. Sectarianism has a long history in Iraq. Even under Saddam, food could be used to express the bigotry of the sectarian divide. He referred to the Shiites of Iraq as "the people of Fessenjen," a slur intended to imply inferiority and to question their origins because the Shiite community favored a Persian-influenced dish that featured a sauce of pomegranate and walnuts. This was a replay of the sectarianism that had bedeviled the country since 1258, when Baghdad's Sunni community had blamed a Shiite minister for opening the doors to the city when the Mongols turned up at the gates. That story was in the grade-school history books.

Iraqis' heightened concern for food had only been sharpened by exile. Claudia Roden, an Egyptian-born food writer and journalist, suggests the connection in the foreword to Richard Tapper and Sami Zubaida's A Taste of Thyme—Culinary Cultures of the Middle East: "There is a lot more to food than eating and cooking. Behind every dish lies a world, a culture, a history. Dishes have social meaning; they have emotional and symbolic significance. Food is about power."

Food's power, if it existed in exile, was in a shared meal, with dishes that conjured up a remembered past of food and friends and home. The diners at the Iraqi restaurants in Damascus were mostly powerless exiles eating from a bitter menu, the losers in the sectarian war that had reshaped Baghdad. The restaurants drew crowds day and night—collectively, the one place in the Syrian capital that was purely Iraq. Mohammed Yahya surveyed the customers—mostly men, with heads bowed over a meal—and dropped his head, too, digging into the hot meal with scoops of bread. Like many of the diners he was trapped in a politically charged international refugee bureaucracy that was frustrating and slow. The year Mohammed was forced into exile, 2007, the U.S. State Department had admitted only 1,608 Iraqis.

The point man at the State Department at the time, Ambassador James Foley, was hand-picked by Secretary of State Condoleezza Rice. He became the official face of the American effort to solve the Iraqi refugee crisis, replacing the ineffective and politically inept Ellen Saurbrey, who had pledged to resettle twenty-five thousand Iraqis in the United States during fiscal year 2007. That figure was used by human rights groups as a measure of dismal failure.

As I looked around the restaurant, I wondered how many others were caught in the same numbers game. Mohammed Yahya had applied for refugee status and resettlement at the United Nations High Commissioner for Refugees office as soon as he arrived in Damascus. He waited in the long line at the processing center on the outskirts of Damascus to make an appointment for the interview. He was told to come back in eight months. When he finally got to his first appointment, during which his case was examined to determine his status as a refugee (i.e., a person with a "well-founded fear of persecution"), the intake officer working for UNHCR told him he would have to wait again. Mohammed was called three months later for a second interview, in May 2008. Again, he was told to wait. The United States accepted 1,141 Iraqi refugees for resettlement in May 2008, the highest number so far for a single month. But there were thousands more still waiting.

Like most other Iraqi refugees, Mohammed relied on his savings to support his family, but after more than a year in Damascus the money was running out. Bread prices had doubled; the Syrian government was phasing out fuel subsidies. For Mohammed, there was the added expense of a new baby on the way. His mood had grown desperate. Despite the claims of improved security in Iraq, he did not dare go back to Baghdad even when his mother unexpectedly died. Mohammed's father warned him that the militiamen in his neighborhood were waiting and expected him to attend the funeral.

I knew of the many hurdles he faced despite having risked his life working for the American project in Iraq. Many Iraqis with similar profiles had been rejected for resettlement in the United States. Part of the problem was the U.S. government's interpretation of the "material support for terrorism" ban, which Congress had expanded as part of the "USA Patriot Act" passed shortly after 9/11. The ban was designed to identify prospective immigrants who had provided support to terrorist groups such as Al Qaeda. However, the one-size-fits-all ban could not anticipate the overwhelming problem for Iraqi refugees: kidnapping. Many Iraqis had paid ransom for the release of a loved one who had been kidnapped by a militia or criminal gang, sometimes for sectarian revenge but often for profit. The U.S. government considered the paying of ransom in such cases—regardless of the circumstances—as constituting "material support" for terrorists, thus barring the surviving family from American resettlement.

The Department of Homeland Security (DHS) was the U.S. agency in charge of interpreting the "material support for terrorism" ban in the Patriot Act, and most of its rulings hued to the strictest possible interpretation. In one case, an Iraqi refugee was on a death list because he had opened a restaurant in the Green Zone in Baghdad in 2003. He and his family enjoyed relative safety while they lived inside the zone catering to American lunch tastes. But in 2004, when he went back to his old neighborhood one day to sell his car, he was kidnapped, interrogated, and tortured with electric shocks, according to his testimony in his UNHCR application form. He acknowledged that he had paid $15,000 to his kidnappers, a ransom for his release.

His UNHCR case file included the notation that the ransom would bar him from U.S. resettlement.

Another even more serious hurdle to U.S. resettlement was a designation that the refugee himself had belonged to a terrorist group. The Patriot Act broadly expanded the definitions here, too. Under the act, a terrorist organization was considered to be any "group of two or more individuals, whether organized or not," who engaged in any form of "terrorist activity." The DHS interviewers had broad latitude to define Iraqi refugees as former terrorists and thus to bar their entry to the United States. And here the bureaucratic reasoning often became bizarre.

One Iraqi refugee claimed he had been threatened after serving as a policeman in Karbala; his training was documented by a California National Guard unit in 2003. A widower with four children, he had applied for resettlement believing that he qualified for U.S. consideration because of his close cooperation with U.S. forces in Iraq. Yet while this ought to have made him a strong candidate, he was rejected. The rejection letter, signed by a U.S. field office director, had a box ticked off that stated, "A waiver is not available for the inadmissibility cited." The citation was "terrorist activity engaged, incited, inspired to up rise against the gov't of Iraq."

The absurdity of the rejection was painful: He was denied resettlement in the United States not because he had participated in an uprising against the current, U.S.-supported, Iraqi government but because he'd been involved in an uprising against the regime of Saddam Hussein after the first Gulf war in 1991. His application for resettlement had listed him as a participant in the 1991 uprising, a mostly Shiite insurrection that had the backing, indeed the encouragement, of U.S. President George H. W. Bush. In the analysis of a bureaucrat in the Homeland Security Department, an Iraqi refugee had been denied entrance to the United States for trying to overthrow

Saddam's regime seventeen years before the Bush administration had finally gotten the job done.

"We've met the enemy. And they are us." That was the judgment of Representative Gary Ackerman, the chair of the Middle East and South Asia subcommittee in the House of Representatives in a hearing on the effects of the Patriot Act on the Iraqi refugee program.

Such stories had become legend in the refugee community. Mohammed knew the discouraging details by heart. So did many others, smoking, sipping sweet tea, eating, and wondering what was next. Our dinner outings were the only times Mohammad Yahya was relatively relaxed. The waiter had filled the table with traditional offerings: a peppery red soup, creamy hummus drizzled with olive oil, grilled eggplant and blackened onions in tomato paste, and a tray of hot, fragrant flat bread. The restaurant's name, Qassim al Kassam Abdul Guss, roughly translated, means "Qassim the butcher who is the father of grilled lamb." *Guss* is the Iraqi Arabic word for shaved spiced lamb meat served on a platter or in a sandwich. At the front of the shop, four man-sized spits of meat, glistening with fat, turned before an open gas-flame roaster. The waiters, in white shirts and black trousers, delivered heaping plates of roasted meat to our table.

"I just taste, I don't cook," said Ahmed al-Qusy, the restaurant manager, as he joined us at the table. "You don't have to be a chef, you just have to know." Qusy seemed an unlikely food authority. He had a thick face and the build of a wrestler with an early paunch, bullet-shaped head, narrow green-yellow eyes, and fat fingers with one gold ring. Qusy had hired the waiters, bakers, and cooks. This was one side of Qusy. There was another side.

Ahmed al-Qusy told me he had been a colonel in Saddam's intelligence service. He'd lost his job in 2003, during the "great sacking" of all Iraqi military personnel ordered by L. Paul Bremer, the American proconsul in Baghdad. Suspected of membership in a Sunni insurgent group, Ahmed said he had been imprisoned by the Americans for eighteen months, first in Abu Ghraib and then in Camp Bucca in southern Iraq. After he was released, he discovered he was on a hit list. "Twice the Shiite militias tried to kill me when I got out of prison. They were coming after the [former] officers. There was a list of names and I was on it." After his father and twin brother were kidnapped and killed, Ahmed left Baghdad and came to Damascus.

"A man must put his faith in his country, his family, and his money. The better alternative, when a man cannot defend any of these things, is to go to a safe place." Ahmed also had found a safe place in Damascus for what I surmised was his crew of Sunni army officers and former insurgents. They had withdrawn from the fight and were grateful for a job serving food to an Iraqi clientele. "I am done with Iraq," said Ahmed al-Qusy.

Mohammed Yahya had worked for the Americans while Ahmed al-Qusy was fighting them, but food had become their common ground. Mohammed had summoned the burly restaurant manager to answer my questions about the grilled lamb on the plate before me. What made this the *Iraqi* version? Why was the dish so different from the Syrian version that Iraqi customers would shun the local variety? I might as well have asked about the difference between Britain's fish and chips and a plate of buttered cod with parsleyed potatoes from France.

"Our grass is greener, our sheep are better, our spices are the best. Nothing is wasted in Iraqi cooking," Ahmed explained as he sketched a crude approximation of a sheep on a napkin. He drew arrows to the parts of the sheep used for each dish—chest, thigh, hindquarter, and the fatted tail. There were no variations. *Quzi* is made from the neck and spine, *tikka* from thigh meat, *pacha* from the head and feet. Ahmed was in charge of buying produce and meat each day, a task that required considerable logistic skills.

"There are areas that we buy from. It is near the Iraqi border, in the Sunni tribal areas that straddle the national frontiers. The grass is greener there, so these animals are the same quality as the ones we get from Iraq." And Ahmed was adamant about the quality of meat available at the Syrian markets. "Syrian sheep have a bad smell!" The bad odor of Syrian sheep seemed unlikely to me; I had often eaten and enjoyed Syrian cuisine, but this was a standard charge against "other" food, an insult that was impossible to refute.

Ahmed oversaw the preparation of the lamb meat by keeping it on ice for three days to "squeeze" the blood. To include lemon, he insisted, was the Iraqi way. But the ingredient that made this dish particularly Iraqi was the 25 percent lamb tail fat that was mixed into the meat. Another lump of lamb fat crowned the roast, bathing the meat and lemon wedges in a shimmering shower of grease as it slowly spun before the fire. Then there were the spices that arrived each day from a market in Baghdad, a complicated mixture that would have been recognizable in the Abbasid era.

"It is a secret ingredient, even I don't know the exact mixture. They call it the Indian spice. It is just for *guss*. It's made in a special shop in Baghdad. But the drivers that bring up the refugees also bring up the spices from Baghdad." Despite all the upheavals in Iraq, and the dangers on the road from the Iraqi capital to this neighborhood restaurant in the suburbs of Damascus, the drivers had never missed a day, delivering human cargo, as well as the all important spices that Iraqis seemingly could not do without.

"If we don't have it—our customers will know—it will still be *guss*, but they will know." Ahmed was passionate about recreating the exact taste of Baghdad, preserving memory. In the back of the restaurant, at the *samoon* oven, Ahmed introduced me to the baker, saying: "His résumé shows that his family has been making *samoon* in Baghdad since 1915!"

Baghdad may have been convulsed by violence, overwhelmed by the American occupation, and transformed by the Shiite-dominated government, but for Ahmed al-Qusy, the ingredients of Baghdad's cuisine would endure—in Damascus.

Were Iraqis always so concerned with food? I put the question again to Sami Zubaida in his London kitchen as he prepared Iraqi tea.

"Yes, always." Zubaida is also an Iraqi exile, but from an older generation. "Iraqis, at home, were concerned with food. This is very urban. Very bourgeois." He poured the dark tea into a cup and then offered hot water to cut the strength, in the Iraqi way.

Sami Zubaida is an expert on the food culture of Iraq and the wider region. He has written books on the subject and delivered academic papers on food culture, tracing the roots of food customs. He is an emeritus professor of sociology at London University, whose specialization is Islamic law, but he seemed to take more pleasure in discussing his research into the origins of food culture.

Masgoof? I asked him about the Tigris River fish split open at the belly and grilled over an open wood fire that I had first tasted in Baghdad.

"You see references to it from Abbasid times. Tenth century. All of the early cookery books, the Arabic manuscripts, are from Iraq. This was aristocratic food in the caliph's palace; this was urban cooking in the Abbasid court."

Pacha, the thick stew made from lamb's head and feet? Baghdad had many restaurants with signs that featured giant sheep heads. "Ah, *pacha*," he said with a chuckle, perhaps recalling some special meal. "This dish is renowned as a breakfast dish. Lots of protein for workers. And it would be heads and feet in a soup. And what tended to happen, the richer people who are out partying all night, drinking, early in the morning, they would go to these places, they would have a late supper, so no hangover."

And on he went, with insight, charm, and a rich laugh, explaining that through Ottoman times and beyond, the observance of food styles and dishes was a feature of Baghdad's urban middle class. Food defined neighborhoods; traditional dishes, often shared between religious and sectarian communities, symbolized the cosmopolitan history of Iraq from the Abbasids to modern times. Zubaida insisted that the true core of the Iraqi spirit is not the country I thought I knew— one sharply divided by communal boundaries and religious conflicts— but, rather, this shared interest in food.

He invited me to an Iraqi restaurant in London, an outing to sample *kibbe*, a traditional Middle Eastern dumpling made with an outer layer of cracked wheat or rice and an inner filling of minced meat, usually lamb. Zubaida ordered the *kibbe batata* not because it was particularly good but because it was a symbol of Iraq's history. *Kibbe batata* had an extra layer of mashed potatoes, an enhancement to the Arabic recipe that was added during the British colonial era in Iraq, an accommodation of British tastes. Food was history.

And there were more examples of food as a map to Iraq's rich past. Zubaida e-mailed me the details of a book from his extensive library, a cookbook from 1946, published by the Iraqi government. *Recipes from Baghdad* opens with an introduction from the Queen Mother of Iraq. "The authors, May H. Beatie, with Bedia Afanan and Renee al-Kabir," were themselves a reflection of Iraq's diversity. Renee al-Kabir was a Jewish notable, Zubaida pointed out. The cookbook was published as a fund-raiser for the Red Cross in Baghdad. Accompanying the list of dishes are details about traditions from all of Iraq's varied communities as well as instructions for the more Western fare preferred by the country's British community. The chapter on measures includes a caveat for non-Iraqi cooks: "It is difficult in Baghdad to obtain the standard measuring cups and measuring spoons which are so generally used in the occident, but it was found that a Players or Gold Flake round 50 cigarette tin, filled level, corresponded to the standard American measuring cup."

I marveled at the cooking directions, which captured a cultural gap between Westerners who read recipes from books and Iraqis who had no need for measuring devices for recipes passed down through generations.

Such elements of historic Iraq—cookbooks, fund-raisers, Jewish notables, a social mingling, people learning the traditions of another sect through sharing holiday foods—reflected a society more than sixty years past, but in Zubaida's optimistic assessment, Iraqi cosmopolitanism still existed. "It is with the exiles, they are the people who are the cosmopolitan Iraq," he said. "It remains in the educated middle classes, in London, in Paris, and now in Amman and Damascus." Iraqis are not natural wanderers like the Lebanese Arabs of the Mediterranean.

Sami Zubaida's expertise in food had led him to early insights into the consequences of the emigrating population. He had warned about the pressure on Baghdad's elite—"under severe attack, and with them the prospect for real democracy"—in published articles and at conferences after the American invasion. But by then, the mass migration of educated Iraqis was already under way. Zubaida went on to point out that this was not the first exodus of Iraq's middle class; it had happened twice in the twentieth century.

"The first was the emigration of the Jewish community in 1950–1951. Until the late 1940s, the Jews were a prominent part of life in Baghdad, where the great majority of an estimated 120,000 Iraqi Jews lived. Jews were government functionaries, professors, businessmen and professionals in medicine, law, journalism and music. Formation of the state of Israel and war with the Arab states made life increasingly hard for the Jews—a great majority emigrated."

A second exodus came during the Saddam era when Shiite merchants were purged. Zubaida pointed out that the Shiites "had replaced the Jews in the markets of the 1950s. Saddam expelled large numbers of Shiites in the 1970s and '80s on the grounds that they were Iranian. Many were wealthy merchants and professionals whose property and businesses were expropriated for the benefit of the regime and its clients."

An exodus was under way again, but in numbers that were far greater than during the previous purges. Many of the latest refugees also came from Iraq's commercial and professional classes, the Sunni technocrats and military families, as well as the remaining Christian minorities. Zubaida had called for the rebuilding of an independent middle class in Iraq. But there was no plan for that, either in Washington or in Baghdad.

Those in the older exile generation were connected to their homeland only by a deep nostalgia. Iraq had been shedding diversity for sixty years: the Jews, the Shiite merchant class. While many of the Shiite merchants expelled by Saddam returned after 2003, now the Sunnis were being driven out, along with other minorities, including the Yazidis and the Christian communities of Greek Orthodox, Armenians, and Mandaeans. Iraq was becoming more of a mono-culture. Tolerance for other religions, other sects, could be proclaimed as public policy and taught in schools, but there was little chance for a real-life lesson of tolerance in Baghdad's recently "unmixed" neighborhoods. Shiite religious officials were clamoring for a new school curriculum that highlighted Shiite history. Iraq's Ministry of Education had rejected an American textbook designed for elementary-school students and translated into Arabic with a lesson that celebrated the notion that people have different religions but are basically all the same.

In Sami Zubaida's memory, food had been the bridge between Iraq's various sects. He had written about a cosmopolitan Baghdad where religious traditions were accompanied by traditional dishes: "Neighbors, attracted by the aromas, had their curiosity satisfied with sample plates being sent between houses, often reciprocated by the recipient's typical food, or some other sweets." But now that a poisonous sectarianism had taken hold and so many people had fled into exile, even food could no longer hold Iraq together.

Zubaida's own experience also showed that exile was often a one-way ticket. Do you dream of going back? I asked him when we first met in London.

"No. Being a Jew, it was never in the cards. Some went back and had to come out again," he said, recalling the early days of the American occupation when there was still hope among the older exile community. "I suppose, myself, I never really thought of Iraq as a possibility. The last time I was there was in 1963. We were okay until then. Then during the '67 war [between Israel and its Arab neighbors], there was terror and persecution of Jews and others. My father was killed. He was arrested and died in detention. Then the rest of my family left." His story was similar to so many I had heard recently in Damascus, Beirut, and Amman. What kind of country will it be? I asked him on that day in London as the tea was brewing. "I dare not think about it," he said, his optimism and his usual laughter failing him.

CHAPTER ELEVEN

MILITIAMEN
COME FROM THE
BEST FAMILIES

In the day-to-day political warfare in the Middle East it was easy to miss the big picture. Other times, the big picture came into focus as sharply as a face in a ski mask at the car window.

"Sunni or Shiite?"

The question followed an insistent knock. The ski mask added menace. A mob of men with automatic rifles, rocket-propelled grenade launchers, pistols, and hand grenades interrogated my driver, whose name was—and you couldn't invent a more appropriate one—Jihad. He had agreed to take me from Beirut to the Syrian border. On a spring day in 2008, our car was forced to stop so the driver could answer one of the most defining questions of the post-Iraq Middle East.

A day earlier, the Lebanese army had closed the main four-lane highway between Lebanon's capital and the border crossing, but Jihad, an experienced driver, knew an alternate mountain route, through

Lebanon's scenic resort towns of Broumana and Zahle, then down the winding roads past the rich agricultural fields of the Bekaa Valley. As we approached Majd al Anjar, a Sunni farming village that occupied a strategic position, I could see young men—*shebab*—standing behind burning tires and armed with heavy clubs and automatic rifles. It was a preview of the chaotic scene at the border a few miles away.

A hundred yards from the border itself, an armed mob controlled the roadway. A farm tractor had been used to push together a large dirt berm, an unofficial checkpoint for the taxis, buses, and private cars that forced passengers to gather their luggage and walk to the border office. Angry and suspicious, the young men from Majd al Anjar shouted, swung their weapons, and leveled their automatic rifles menacingly from behind the dirt berm. Undisciplined and leaderless, they would soon swarm over passengers and drivers alike.

"Sunni or Shiite?" another gunman hissed as Jihad unloaded my luggage from the trunk. Jihad, unfailingly polite, released a breath when he answered a second time. Jihad and I had driven together many times before. I knew him to be a religious man; he prayed five times a day. However, the question he was being asked was not a test of his Islamic devotion but of his sectarian loyalty. Lebanon had adopted the checkpoint ritual and the threatening sectarian language of Iraq. There were even more direct connections with Iraq.

The glowering men at the Lebanese border were from a farming village that had dispatched scores of young Sunni men to fight or volunteer for suicide operations against the U.S.-backed Shiite government in Baghdad. The village was "jihadi central"—a recruiting center for Al Qaeda and a well-known smuggling hub for "foreign" jihadis on the way to Iraq. The religious leaders of Majd al Anjar preached a radical ideology that declared Shiite Muslims to be infidels, and therefore targets to be killed.

The sons of Majd al Anjar were prepared to fight to restore Sunni supremacy in Iraq against what they saw as the aberration of an Arab

Shiite government under American patronage. But the events of that month, May 2008, revealed a more striking parallel: As in Iraq, in Lebanon the Sunni Muslim order was failing and being displaced by a more powerful Shiite political organization—in this case, under the patronage of Iran.

The fury on the Lebanese border had been stoked a few days earlier when Hezbollah, Lebanon's Shiite militia, had closed down the road to Beirut's airport and then swiftly taken control of the streets of West Beirut—humiliating the amateur Sunni militias imported from villages in the north and recently armed by Sunni political powers in the capital. On the border, the young Sunnis of Majd al Anjar were not connected to Lebanon's traditional Sunni elite, the militias, or the political parties that claimed to represent Sunni interests. This mob had seized the roadway entirely on its own in retaliation for Hezbollah's airport closure. As soon as news of the border takeover reached Beirut, no Shiite drivers were to be found heading for the border. Jihad was a Sunni. I made sure of that before we left Beirut, a question I had never needed to ask him before.

He and I joined the line of people trudging toward the border post, dragging luggage over the dirt path through the berm, past the snack shops and currency exchange booths, past gun-toting older men sitting on plastic chairs, past young boys who had been attracted by the electricity of expected violence in the air. The Lebanese army was stationed nearby, down an alley, protected behind the concrete wall of an empty building. I could see soldiers perched on top of armored personnel carriers, relaxed, smoking cigarettes. The uniforms stayed on the sidelines watching the anarchy nearby. They made no move to unblock the road or confront the roadside Sunni militia. The border police had retreated to the passport control office for protection from the mayhem they expected to break out at any moment. They solemnly stamped my travel document without looking up. The Lebanese state still notionally controlled the official border with

Syria, a few miles away. Syrian cab drivers, usually idling on the other side of the border, were allowed to wait on the Lebanese side. In Middle East fashion, border officials saw a way to ease the chaos. The gunmen had stopped Lebanese cab drivers from crossing the makeshift dirt berm, so that opened up a business opportunity for the Syrian cabbies and a crucial service for stranded Lebanese passengers. "Syria? Syria?" the drivers whispered, hailing passenger with a promise of escape from Lebanon's sectarian storm.

The blockade, brimming with potential violence, lasted for a few days during which, for the most part, the border stayed open. The Lebanese army eventually forced the angry young men back to Majd al Anjar.

"In a tribal system, the perception of power is more important than power. So you have to bang on the table," said Timur Goksel, a former UN official and now a lecturer at the American University in Beirut. He confirmed that the border demonstration was one way to bang the table, but the banging was the sound of defeat. The Sunnis of Lebanon were losing. Hezbollah and Lebanon's Shiite community had gained in the latest round and would continue to do so, even while losing parliamentary seats in a national election in 2009 but retaining the power to dominate the Lebanese government. The confrontation on the streets of West Beirut raised fundamental questions about Lebanon's future and its identity. Lebanon's political institutions, the "democratic sectarian system" on which the country was built, had been strained, perhaps to the breaking point.

"The Shiites want more power and they see you have to fight to get it with a gun," Goksel said, sadly. Many of his students had joined in the fight, he told me. "Many of the militiamen go to the American University in Beirut. These kids come from the best families." I had trouble envisioning the gunmen on the streets of Beirut sitting in the conflict management class that Goksel taught.

Free-wheeling Beirut did not look or feel like a tribal society. The old Levantine spirit, the Lebanese model of sectarian mixing, still seemed alive; Beirut was the bridge-city between East and West. On Hamra Street, the commercial district, Internet cafés, the Starbucks coffee shop, and late-night bars and nightclubs catered to the various tastes of the city. But Lebanon was built on a sectarian system institutionalized by the French, the colonial power until World War II. In Lebanon's case, the entire country—from the Mediterranean coastal cities to the Lebanon mountains to the fertile Bekaa Valley—was carved out of Syrian territory, devised to provide a protective state for Maronite Christians in the predominantly Muslim Middle East. In 1943, the National Pact required that both the president and the army commander must be Maronite Christians. The prime minister would be a Sunni; the speaker of Parliament, a Shiite Muslim; and the deputy speaker, a Greek Orthodox Christian. The agreement also called for the Maronite Christians to accept Lebanon as an Arab rather than a Western country, and for the Muslims of Lebanon to abandon aspirations to unite with Syria. The power distribution and Christian dominance reflected demographics confirmed by a census carried out in the 1930s, but the population of Lebanon had changed dramatically since then. Shiite Muslims claimed they were now the single largest sectarian group and demanded what they saw as a fair share of power. "Iraq rules" were operating in Lebanon: Sectarian identity offered protection where the central state was weak.

In the summer of 2008, Lebanon had become another version of postwar Iraq: boiling sectarian tensions, neighborhood militias, and the threat of a civil-sectarian war. But Lebanon was also part of a regional power struggle, another front in the proxy war for influence between the United States and Iran—one that would continue long past the outcome of this particular, but instructive, confrontation. The outcomes in Lebanon and Iraq were linked.

In Lebanon, rising tensions had kicked off after a walkout of Shiite cabinet ministers representing Hezbollah. With Shiite interests no longer represented, Hezbollah declared the remaining rump government illegitimate. Some state institutions ceased to function. The remaining cabinet, along with the Sunni prime minister, retreated to the Grand Seriel, the refurbished Ottoman-era government headquarters in central Beirut. Barricaded, government officials lived and worked in the Seriel, 24/7, conducting government business behind barbed wire and armed guards. Hezbollah raised the stakes by mounting a mass demonstration, creating a tent-city in downtown Beirut, shutting down the name-brand shops, restaurants, and wine bars in the central business district for more than a year.

The May 2008 showdown began over a private telecommunication network, a fiber-optic landline system that gave Hezbollah's military command a secure, unmonitored communications infrastructure from the south of the country into the capital. The communications system was a strategic asset in any future war with Israel. The U.S.-backed Lebanese government issued a direct challenge to Hezbollah's state within a state by pledging to dismantle the phone network as well as a Hezbollah-controlled camera monitoring system at the Beirut airport. Hezbollah's charismatic leader Hassan Nasrallah gave his response to the government ultimatum in a news conference two days later. The international media were notified to show up for security checks at 3 P.M., the Lebanese media at 3:30. In front of a giant television screen, a Hezbollah official counted down the start time—five, four, three, two, one. At exactly four o'clock Nasrallah appeared "live" on screen for the gathered media and on Al Manar, Hezbollah's television station that broadcasts throughout the region. Hezbollah's information campaign was as disciplined as the street battle that followed. Smiling and relaxed, Nasrallah, speaking from a secure underground bunker in Beirut said to be equipped with an air filtration system and a dedicated fiber-optic link, rebuked the Lebanese government. "They talked peace and gave us war," he said. "Those who try to arrest us, we will arrest them. Those who shoot at us, we will shoot at them. The hand raised against us, we will cut it off."

An hour later, Saad Hariri, the leader of the Future party, as the Sunni political movement was called, gave the government's response. His message was overshadowed by the unmistakable symbolism of the first few minutes of his live television appearance: In contrast to the confident and punctual Nasrallah, the first broadcast images of Hariri caught him off-guard looking away from the camera with the sound cut off.

Hariri's Future party was at the center of the March 14 governing coalition, which takes its name from the day of a massive public demonstration that helped pressure Syria to end three decades of heavy-handed influence. The spontaneous demonstrations that followed the assassination of Rafiq Hariri, the popular former prime minister, were fueled by the belief of many Lebanese that the Syrians were responsible for Hariri's death. Faced with popular anger in Lebanon and international pressure, Syria pledged to withdraw all of its forces by April, 30, 2005, and agreed to a United Nations monitoring team to verify the pullout. By 2008, the March 14 coalition was backed by the United States and Saudi Arabia in an effort to keep formal political power in Lebanon from passing into the hands of Hezbollah and patrons Iran and Syria, an effort that faltered on the streets of the capital.

Within hours of the dueling political television broadcasts, Hezbollah Shiite fighters swept though Sunni West Beirut, taking the contest to the streets. I was staying in a hotel near Hamra Street, where heavy gunfire was so close I could smell it as the hotel manager herded his guests into the basement gym for protection against bullets and flying glass. I could see Lebanese on the balconies of apartment buildings that overlooked Hamra Street watching the show.

These events reinforced that theater was an important part of Middle East politics. Sometimes I would imagine the warlords and the gunman meeting off-stage somewhere for a laugh, high-fiving each other over a particular innovation in political theater. Guns, theater, and masquerade. The ski-masked young men at the Lebanese border had a flair for performance. Hezbollah's precise timing at news conferences was a theatrical gesture meant to convey discipline and control. Some of the heaviest fighting was on Friday, the traditional day of prayer. This, too, was a metaphor.

There was a moment of high drama in the hotel gym when Hezbollah's armed men charged down the stairs to confront our group of tired and frightened guests. The uniformed investigators thought we might be harboring a sniper, and came to question us armed with rocket-propelled grenade launchers and stern faces.

Following the pounding of heavy boots and loud voices, full-uniform, clean-shaven, Hezbollah professionals, frontline fighters from the south, hurtled down the steps and discovered our motley crew, including two professors, an American journalist, a Colombian businessman, an Indian economist, and the hotel manager's wife and two young sons—all of us standing in the mirrored basement gym around the weight benches and running machines. In the tumult, the soldiers separated the women from the men, confiscated our cellphones, and took a long hard look at us as we blinked back at them after a long and sleepless night. Then they marched up the stairs to resume fighting outside. A half-hour later, the unit commander came back to our group to apologize. Sorry to bother you, he said, as shells rained down on the street outside. Hezbollah's sweep into Beirut was a show of force intended for a Lebanese audience, the Sunni power structure of Beirut, and the wider Arab world. We were protected and irrelevant bystanders.

In this way, on the streets of West Beirut, Hezbollah demonstrated that it was the most powerful political force in Lebanese politics. Hezbollah's success was Iran's success. Within a week, Lebanon's warring factions agreed to formal negotiations, flying separately to Doha, Qatar, a neutral place for talks. On the airport road, ordinary Lebanese demonstrated their mental fatigue with placards that read: "If you don't agree, don't come back!" But an agreement was hardly in doubt. Waleed Jumblatt, the Lebanese leader of the Druze and a well-known political weather vane in the country, called the U.S. embassy before he left for Doha and told the ambassador: "The U.S. has failed in Lebanon," adding, "We have to wait and see the new rules which Hezbollah, Syria, and Iran will set. They can do what they want."

The Arab League and the emir of Qatar sponsored talks that secured Hezbollah's role in a government that included Western-leaning politicians, which allowed the Party of God a veto in any decisions with which it did not agree. The West, if it respected its own allies in Lebanon, would have to accept the political legitimacy of Hezbollah. It was a huge prize for a group that had been portrayed as an Iranian-backed terrorist organization. By 2009, the British government expressed a willingness to resume contacts with the political wing of Hezbollah—suspended since 2005, while the United States and Israel denied such a thing existed separate from the military one. Hezbollah had brilliantly divided the Western allies. In government, Hezbollah had a blocking veto for every vote in Lebanon's cabinet. Lebanon had been without a head of state for six months after nineteen failed parliamentary votes. The new rules provided for an emergency session of Parliament to elect a president, a Christian army general who enjoyed cordial relations with Damascus. Lebanon had averted a sectarian civil war, but the Doha agreement, as it was called, recognized a new power balance in Lebanon and in the region. Hezbollah had prevailed along with its ally and patron Iran. Without waging war, Iran had skillfully expanded its political influence in places that before 2003 had been under Arab sway, including Lebanon, Iraq, and Palestine. The Arabs—above all the Sunni powers—had lost ground everywhere. Even the radical Sunni movements, Hamas and the Muslim Brother-hood, were increasingly dependent on Tehran. Egypt's Hosni Mubarak and Saudi Arabia's King Abdullah were furious about Iran's growing reach into the Arab heartland but what could they do about it? The American invasion that had removed Iraq from the balance-of-power equations on the Sunni side had tilted the region toward Tehran. The Sunni powers shuddered to think of living under the embrace of Shiite mullahs with nuclear arms.

Two days after my basement encounter with Hezbollah, back on the highway to Damascus, the open sectarian warfare of Lebanon seemed to have given way to the open roads of Syria, the landscape marked by billboards depicting the Syrian president, Bashar al-Assad. It was a different world, or was it?

Assad was well aware that he ruled over a Sunni majority in-creasingly uneasy with the Iranian alliance at a time of heightened Sunni-Shiite tensions. On the day of Hezbollah's triumph in Doha, in a piece of matching theater—a coordinated media campaign—announcements from Damascus, Tel Aviv, and Ankara confirmed that indirect talks had started between Syria and Israel under the auspices of the Turks. Bashar al-Assad, Iran's sole Arab ally, was look-ing to cut his own deal. How would Tehran react? In another turn of the Middle East kaleidoscope, the Syrian-Iranian alliance no longer appeared quite so secure.

Assad was rewarded for his role in Lebanon and for the indirect talks with Israel. Within six weeks Assad would be in Paris, the guest of French President Nicholas Sarkozy, an invitation that brought Syria and the Syrian president in from the cold of American-imposed isolation.

The media photographs of the Paris trip focused on Asma al-Assad, a stunning thirty-three-year-old blond in haute couture, with short-cropped and conspicuously uncovered stylish hair. With her husband Bashar, in well-tailored dark suits, smiling, basking in his international rehabilitation, she presented the cosmopolitan face of Syria. Sarkozy had invited the Syrian president to a summit of Mediterranean leaders. The Mediterranean group was the French president's invention: He determined it would include Syria along with Israel.

In effect, the invitation recognized that attempts to isolate Syria—U.S. policy since 2000—had failed. If there was ever a serious plan for Syria to be next in the Middle East dominoes of falling dictators, that plan was off the books. As the Bush administration faded, there was a revival in the belief that Syria was a difficult but necessary player in the Middle East with a role in the interlocking conflicts. France was the first Western power to make the strategy public. The Bush era, marked by revolutionary American power, unilaterally and militarily driven to remake Arab and Islamic lands, was ending. With the strategic mistakes in Lebanon, Syria, and Iraq, the United States had actually weakened its ability to shape events. The French president defined the new approach. "How can you make peace if you don't talk to people with different opinions?" he asked, defending his decision to invite the Assads to the Bastille Day celebrations in the City of Lights.

Bashar al-Assad had reaped his rewards for conducting indirect peace talks with Israel through Turkish mediators, for launching relations with the new Iraqi state (being one of the few Arab leaders to do so), pledging to open an embassy in Lebanon, and, for the first time, recognizing the Lebanese state. Hosting Iraqi refugees also played a part in Assad's rehabilitation in European capitals. He had opened his country to United Nations aid workers, international nongovernment agencies, and, eventually, American officials from the Department of Homeland Security. Syria's hospitality and willingness to assume the economic burden for the care of the human crisis spawned by the war in Iraq had paid off. A trip to Paris was Assad's prize. He had earned the respect formerly reserved for his father, and shed the image of an heir that was a diluted version of his father's hardier stock. In Paris, the Assads presented the promise of a more modern Middle East, while at home his secret police still detained democracy advocates and the courts still sentenced them to jail. Assad had gained a great deal at very little inconvenience to Syria, and without any risk to his personal rule.

For Omar Amiralay, a part of Syria's imperiled "civil society," it was hard to give credit to Bashar as long as democratic activists remained in jail. "Yes, Syria is changing," Omar said, shrugging. At times, it did seem that Syria lurched in a positive direction, only to tack back to the old ways. Major reforms in the judiciary, the banking system, and the media were still on hold, and there was a complete absence of any legal protections for Syrian citizens. But even Amiralay, long an opponent of Baathism in Syria, acknowledged that an era was ending. "Baathism has become a fiction. It is dead," he said. And with the death of Baathism, the ideology of pan-Arab nationalism was ending, too—a "mercy killing," according to Amiralay. When Assad agreed to open an embassy in Lebanon, a step toward establishing diplomatic relations between the two countries for the first time, he had tacitly declared the borderless Baathist dream of Greater Syria over.

"We have been living with the consequences of the end of the Ottoman empire and the decisions of the British and French," Amiralay added, referring to the French diplomat Francois Georges-Picot and to the Briton Sir Mark Sykes, who in 1915–1916 negotiated an agreement that created the French and British spheres of influence in the Middle East that, in turn, led to the drawing of colonial borders to determine Western control of oil. For ninety years, Syrians had rejected the colonial land-grab, the border-drawing exercise in the 1920s that imposed boundaries to suit Western oil interests.

Yet now "Syria has taken the last step in executing the Sykes-Picot treaty," Amiralay affirmed. "For the first time, Syria recognizes that Sykes-Picot is real. They never have [before]. There is still the point to define the borders. Then we can say that Sykes-Picot is complete. Syria was always the last holdout." For generations of Syrians the grand idea of Pan-Arabism—a Syria larger than its Western-imposed borders—was part of their identity. As for Lebanon, the Syrian saying "two people in one country" was no more.

Baathism suffered a violent end in Iraq when the Americans arrived in Baghdad, and it withered at a slower pace in Syria. Pan-Arabism was also failing. It had not been able to give a single identity to the regions' various tribes and groups nor deliver a single victory in war or peace with Israel. Instead, political Islam was the newly favored brand. Syria's stability, rooted in a secular ideology, could not be guaranteed in a region that was straining under sectarian animosities.

In October 2008, I was invited to a dinner in the Syrian hills by an old friend. He is a private Syrian citizen, but also an insider within the Assad regime. I was never really sure how far "inside" he was, but we always met when I came to Damascus. That is how it works in the Middle East, especially in Syria: relationships built over time, long discussions that eventually reveal a picture of a regime as secretive as the old Kremlin, a regime where power is confined to a handful of people, mostly family and loyalists. My friend had been right about many things. He had shared his fears about Syria's growing bonds with Tehran. Damascus certainly needed the Persian investments. In the 1980s and 1990s, Syria had one of the fastest-growing populations in the world. The children born in those decades were now flooding the job markets, and the economy would have to expand to accommodate them at a time when the Syrian oil fields were running dry. But the strategic relationship worked mostly in Iran's favor, isolating Arab and Sunni Syria from the rest of the Arab world. Historic ties with Saudi Arabia and Egypt were at an all-time low. My Syrian friend also worried about the rise of militant Islam in the shadows of his country, a dangerous blowback from Iraq. For Syria, Iraq had been a convenient place to dispose of its most fervent homegrown jihadists, a short-term success, which now strained the ability of the Syrian intelligence agencies to keep tabs on the determined militants. My friend had often told me about the Syrian president's push to open an unofficial negotiating channel with Israel. I discounted his early revelations as self-serving propaganda until the meetings became public. I looked forward to his dinner invitation and to his "insider" view of the country.

The evening's special guest, Tom Dine, was a most unlikely visitor to Damascus. Once a Peace Corps volunteer in the Philippines, he had become a cool practitioner in the uses of political power. Dine was well known in Washington. In 1980, he took over as the executive director of AIPAC, the American-Israel Public Affairs Committee. Over the next thirteen years he transformed the pro-Israel lobby into a major political force. The *Wall Street Journal* reported in 1991 that AIPAC worked in tandem with the George H. W. Bush administration to pass the congressional vote authorizing the first Gulf war. Dine told the *Journal*, "If you sit on the sidelines you have no voice." In 2002, he used that voice again, joining Richard Perle and other neoconservatives to form the Committee for the Liberation of Iraq, urging President George W. Bush to overthrow Saddam Hussein. Now, he was in Damascus, his second trip, and he had a very different cause. "Our mission is to normalize Syrian relations. In a normal relationship you have two embassies with ambassadorial leadership and political and economic relations." Dine explained that a group of Americans and Syrians had come up with a strategic plan to normalize relations within a year, reversing the Bush administration's isolationist policies.

Dine now headed the American-Syrian working group that was the brainchild of an organization called Search for Common Ground. The Washington-based group had a long history in international conflict resolution and had reached out to him to head a new initiative on Syria. Dine's working group comprised eight high-level people from each country, including former American ambassadors as well as advisors to the Syrian government.

The dinner in Damascus was at the home of economist Samir Seifan, a Syrian member of the working group. In the cool night air, in the hills outside the capital, Seifan's wife served an outdoor feast of Syrian specialties. The bonds of understanding and common purpose were reinforced with glasses of *arak* and cigars. The American elections were a still a month away, but the conversation centered on candidate Barack Obama. Could he win? The Syrians were skeptical. Would he change the American approach toward Syria? Could Obama lift the economic sanctions imposed on Syria? Dine gave an honest assessment, which he shared with me later, reflecting on the dinner that night and subsequent meetings with the working group. He believed discussions had to be based on honesty and truth. "This is not Sunday school. The U.S.-Syrian relationship is very, very bad," he said. "It is quite sour. I don't try to sugar it up, because if we don't deal with the six issues—Iraq, Iran, Hezbollah, Hamas, Lebanon, and Israel—things don't have a good chance of improving."

For months before he took the assignment, Tom Dine had been driven by a simple but disruptive belief. "I was furious with Bush politics of isolation toward Iran and Syria. I had felt for a long time that it was unproductive. It was producing nothing for the United States," he said, a judgment that had become widely shared by Washington's policy elites. But Dine decided to do something about it, in the waning months of the Bush administration, by using his longtime Washington connections and considerable organizing skills to reverse the corrosive "big stick" policies of the Bush years and add more "speaking softly." He hoped to keep the dialogue open until a new administration was in place.

"I'm not doing this for Syria. I'm doing this for the United States. This is how I define American interests. Now, here I am. I've spent the last decades involved in frontline advancement of democratic institution building and I am quite aware of the lack of human rights in Syria. But one step at a time."

He had spent more than a decade making Israel's case in Washington and felt his views were in line with important players in Israeli politics. "The most credible institution in the country is for it. It's the military, it's the defense minister, it's former military personnel who realize that the name of the game is Iran, so you go for a treaty with Syria."

The political atmosphere had changed considerably since Dine's first tentative meetings in Syria. When it took office, the Obama administration moved quickly to change the tone, if not the policies, reaching out to friends and foes alike. The Egyptians and the Saudis were on board, talking to the Syrians again because of three "I"s: Iran, Israel, and Iraq. Iran's growing influence in the region, the uncertainties over the U.S. withdrawal from Iraq, and the regional reality of the new right-wing government in Israel had put a premium on Arab solidarity.

It was no secret that the subtext for these warm embraces was to distance Damascus from Tehran. That is what the Saudis wanted. That is what the Obama administration wanted, too. The polarization in the region—driven, in part, by the Bush administration—had pushed Syria ever closer to an Iranian embrace. But what was the price to woo Damascus away from the thirty-year alliance?

The thick vellum invitation arrived unexpectedly in my New York mailbox from the Syrian ambassador, Imad Moustapha, in Washington. I was invited to celebrate Syrian National Day on April 17, 2009. It was a sumptuously catered coming-out party, a sign that Syria was a player in Washington again, the first time in eight years that the Syrian embassy had organized a high-profile reception, since the first year of the Bush administration when it was clear that the RSVP response would be only regrets from State Department officials.

In the ballroom at a hotel near the capitol, the guests were a mix of Arab diplomats, media celebrities, political analysts, and consultants. The Syrian ambassador basked in the success of a guest list that included diplomats from Iraq, Lebanon, and Saudi Arabia, a reflection of the changing tone in the region as well as in Washington. But the most significant guests were from the top rungs of the U.S. State Department: Fredric Hof, a regional expert who worked with George Mitchell, the president's envoy to the Middle East, and Jeffrey Feltman, acting assistant secretary of state for Near Eastern Affairs and former ambassador to Lebanon. Such high-level American officials at a Syrian-sponsored function would have been unthinkable during the Bush administration. Feltman had been an outspoken critic of the Syrian regime when he served as ambassador to Lebanon during the Bush years. He was often vilified in the Syrian state-controlled media for what Damascus considered "meddling" in Lebanese affairs, yet he was now President Obama's representative at the reception and warmly shook hands with the Syrian ambassador at the front-door reception line. Ambassador Imad Moustapha smiled just as brightly. Times had certainly changed.

Candidate Obama had pledged to reinstate diplomatic relations with Syria, and his administration was making good on that promise— one carrot at a time. The first carrot was unmistakable. The U.S.

sanctions imposed relentlessly by the Bush administration had been keenly felt by Syria's state-run airlines. Some of Syria's aging domestic fleet was grounded, impossible to repair and too dangerous to fly. Spare parts for the American-made Boeing 747s were off-limits due to U.S. sanctions. In one of the first gestures toward Damascus, the United States agreed to allow Boeing to resume selling spare parts to Syrian airlines.

The thaw was a necessary demonstration of the Obama doctrine, loosely defined as seizing on areas of cooperation while respecting that countries have interests that may put them at odds with the United States. Syria was being used as a test of the formula. The new administration read Syria's position in the region correctly, as a lever in the balance between the rising power of Iran and the Sunni Arab states. Assad had presented himself as a lever, too, but he was not playing by American rules. Why should he? Assad's alliances with Iran, Hezbollah, and Hamas had proved a winning strategy, allowing Syria to play above its weight. Syria—a country with inadequate resources, a weak military, a dismal record in governance and human rights—held cards in all the major regional games. Damascus couldn't shape events, but it could stand in the way, a spoiler in the Middle East, where the conflicts were interconnected.

What are the odds that the conflicts in the Middle East can be settled? Certainly not within the four- or eight-year time frame for an American president, even one who grasped the core political conflicts, enjoyed enormous popularity and legitimacy, and was willing to dig in at the beginning of his presidency, rather than wait for the waning days of an administration in search of a legacy, the practice of his two predecessors. Drawing Israel back into a commitment to open talks with Damascus was the most promising choice in a difficult Middle East agenda for President Barack Obama. The issues were clear— withdrawal, security, water, borders—and the gaps could be bridged.

The two sides had come tantalizingly close in negotiations under the Clinton administration in 2000, and again in the Turkish-brokered indirect talks that stalled over Israel's 2008 military campaign in Gaza. Renewed peace talks would change the dynamics of the region; a peace treaty could realign the region's alliances and confront Hezbollah, Hamas, and Iran with hard choices. In the interconnected conflicts of the region, changing the dynamics on the Israel-Syria track was a step toward the "Grand Bargain" with Iraq's neighbors that Washington's foreign policy community believed was the only way to ensure stability after the U.S. withdrawal. Of course, the American president would have to push Israel and Syria further than both countries were willing to go. But if President Obama's main concern was Iran, it made sense to start by sitting down with Syria.

CHAPTER TWELVE

FAR AWAY

In June 2009, the United Nations High Commissioner for Refugees registration office in the Damascus neighborhood of Kafr Sousa was the place to observe the political failures in Baghdad, accommodated by the United Nations and the continuing generosity of the Syrian government. For the UN workers, the procedures had settled into the numbing routine of a crisis that had gone on too long. Every Tuesday, the UN workers were confronted by a disorderly mob, mostly women, glistening with sweat and anxiety, their voices clamoring furiously whenever a United Nations official appeared. Hands shot up clutching well-worn documents, waved as flags of family calamity. Tuesdays were the one day of the week when they could wait in line to speak to a United Nations official face to face. For some, circumstances had not changed since the last time I had waded into this crowd of exiles six months earlier.

Iraq remained the top country of origin for asylum applications for four years running, and while UNHCR had referred more than eighty thousand Iraqis for resettlement, acceptance by a resettlement country remained slow and unpredictable: It could take years. In the thickened crowd, English speakers pushed themselves forward. "I am here for my brother and I came here to help him with his situation," said Najah Rasheed abruptly, as if I already knew the intimate details of her separated family. She had been resettled to Canada. When? I couldn't be sure. She believed her personal appeal would improve her brother's chances to join her. "He's been suffering for five years, imagine," she said indignantly, in a practiced tone usually reserved for the United Nations officials sitting on plastic chairs at the head of the line. Many here had given up on the Middle East and wanted to join family members already resettled to Sweden, Australia, or the United States, and had come to plead the case.

Fatin Franscis had a more modest request. An Iraqi Christian resigned to permanent exile in Syria, Fatin wanted a monthly stipend in addition to the food rations that the UN awarded to the neediest cases. "My kids are working, and I work sometimes. They give us food, but it's not good. It's not fit for animals. We throw it away or we sell it." The Iraqi exile community had settled into a long-term, dependent wait. I asked if there were recent arrivals in line. "Yes, of course," Fatin insisted; she came here every week and the newcomers stood out. "It's still hard there. It's not good in Iraq now. They are still killing people."

A story of murder, decapitation to be more precise, brought Motah Fatah al-Saleh to stand in this line at the office in Kafr Sousa. A Sunni Arab from Baghdad, he was new to the Tuesday routine, still awkward in recounting the details of the events that compelled him to leave home. He claimed his mother had been beheaded in her kitchen. "She had been warned to stop asking questions about her kidnapped sons," said Saleh, as if to explain the gruesome death that seemed to him as predictable as the weather. His mother had taken her complaints to a government office in Baghdad, Saleh told me. This was a new twist to the old threat-and-murder routine in Iraq. There was a government office for complaints, but push too hard, get too close to criminals who had the power to stop an investigation, and the results were the same as during the worst days of the civil war.

Philippe Leclerc, the acting director of the UNHCR office, verified the broader trends in the exile community. "When you talk to the refugees, 90 percent do not intend to go back in the near future," he confirmed. More than two hundred thousand Iraqis were still registered with UNHCR but there were tens of thousands more Iraqis living in Damascus who had no links with UNHCR. Syrian officials claimed that 1.2 million remained in the country, based on the number of residency permits, but the exile community had become more transient: One member of the family, a father or a brother, would be sent back to Baghdad to collect a pension or back pay, or to work for a few months to support the extended family exiled in Syria. "The numbers are down from six months ago, because there is mobility in part of the population," said Leclerc. "There is a substantial group going back and forth. The perception among most Iraqis, let's keep options open. The trust-building is not there."

The traffic between Baghdad and Damascus worked like a lung, in and out, according to the rise and fall of violence. The border traffic came to a halt in the spring of 2009 when a prominent politician, the head of the largest Sunni Arab bloc in Parliament, was shot in the head by a teenaged boy in the West Baghdad neighborhood of Yarmouk. Harith al-Obeidi was a Sunni leader of unusual moderation and civility. A university law professor and a human rights activist, he was gunned down while giving a sermon at Friday prayers in one of the most heavily guarded neighborhoods in the capital. With his death, even the transient exiles decided it was best to stay in Syria and wait.

Obeidi represented the best hope for Sunni reconciliation with Iraq's Shiite leadership. He shared Prime Minister Nouri al-Maliki's view that Iraq would be better off when the Americans left the country,

although he was more direct in his blame. "The occupation is responsible for every crime and the death of every citizen in Iraq" was his
often quoted remark, a strident rebuke that raised suspicion he was
aligned with the Sunni insurgency that led to a raid on his house by
U.S. forces in 2005. But Obeidi's "insurgency" was entirely a political
one. He campaigned for the disarmament of militias, Sunni and Shiite
alike, and for the restructuring of the army along nationalist lines without regard to sectarian labels. His most vocal campaign was against
Iraq's treatment of Sunni prisoners, and his outspoken criticism of
Maliki's government ministers strained relations between the two
men. On the day of his death, Obeidi had railed against the lack of
accountability and justice in Prime Minister Maliki's Iraq to a full
house of Sunnis at the mosque. He was waging a losing political battle
for a general amnesty for Sunni prisoners and a greater role for Sunni
politicians in the post-2003 political system. In his role as the deputy
chairman of Parliament's human rights committee, he represented
Sunni Arab families who had lost sons within the government prison
system. On the day before his death, he had called for an investigation
of the ministers of defense and of the interior in Maliki's cabinet,
blaming them for sectarian violence and appalling prison conditions.

In his final public oration, Obeidi thundered against the forgotten
Sunni prisoners in Iraq's jails. "Nobody knows about him except God!"
he said, a moment before a teenager somehow slipped through the
ring of guards and shot him at point-blank range.

Harith al-Obeidi's death was a national tragedy. Iraq lost an effective
and trusted voice for reconciliation. Maliki, whose relations with Obeidi
were always strained, immediately condemned the attack, claiming
that whoever shot the Sunni politician was trying to spread sectarian
violence, and ordered a televised state funeral, the only one since the
U.S.-led invasion in 2003. Obeidi had more power in death than in
life to unify Baghdad's warring political factions. Iraqi politicians—

Shiite, Sunni, and Kurd—gathered inside the protected Green Zone to show their respect. A military honor guard escorted the casket to the main Sunni cemetery near the Abu Hanifa mosque in northern Baghdad. In Cairo, the Arab League noted the death of a "loud voice of moderation and a prominent Iraqi leader," a recognition that silencing a voice of reason had consequences on the streets of Beirut, Damascus, and Amman.

Iraq's sectarian war had largely ended by the time of Harith al-Obeidi's assassination. The Sunni Arabs and Iraqi Christians accepted defeat in the war on the streets, but another struggle was under way— a political power struggle that was no less perilous and continued to create more exiles. Sunni leaders were still angling for real power. The Shiite parties were determined not to yield it. Iraq and the region would not be stable until this phase of the political battle was resolved.

As a candidate for president, Barack Obama aimed to measure an end to displacement and exile as a benchmark of Iraq's long-term stability. President Obama linked the refugee crisis again when he outlined his plan for an accelerated U.S. withdrawal from Iraq. At Camp LeJeune in Jacksonville, North Carolina, he told the Marines: "These men, women, and children are a living consequence of this war and a challenge to stability in the region, and they must become a part of Iraq's reconciliation and recovery." Obama said that America had a strategic and moral responsibility to resolve the crisis, "because there are few more powerful indicators of lasting peace than displaced citizens returning home." The president raised the issue with Prime Minister Maliki in the spring of 2009, on his first overseas trip since his election. The displacement-exile crisis was unfinished business that had become more urgent with the looming deadline of American withdrawal. Obama's plan for a "responsible" withdrawal included a resolution for the refugees and the displaced. But time was running out and there was no definitive plan.

Adnan al-Shourifi knew who to blame. Shourifi, an Iraqi bureaucrat, had been on the job for two years when I arrived at his office in Damascus. He already knew the importance of assigning guilt to deflect criticism, seemingly a necessary skill for Arab officials of Shourifi's rank. He was the commercial attaché at the Iraqi embassy in Damascus, in charge of organizing the cars, buses, and plane tickets to entice Iraqi exiles back home. He had to sell the deal that included free transportation to Baghdad and a cash payment of about $850 per family. This was an update of the disastrous 2007 government plan that ended after only one bus convoy arrived in Baghdad. In the updated version, exiles had to cancel their Syrian residency permits as well as their refugee status with UNHCR, giving up the right to return to Syria or to qualify for resettlement. But this government program had stalled as well. Shourifi had an elaborate explanation for why Iraqis still refused to go home in meaningful numbers.

I had met Adnan al-Shourifi a year earlier, when the Maliki government first mounted an initiative to get Iraqi exiles to go home. He assured me then that the majority of the exile population would embrace the government program. Indeed, he told me that all of the Iraqi exiles would be home within months, a prediction wildly off the mark. A year later, he had a long list of culprits for the failure that began with UNHCR and the U.S. government for resettling thousands more Iraqis in America and Europe than the year before. "The UNHCR gave too many promises that Iraqis would be resettled [abroad]. So people stayed here. Even if the Iraqi government solved the problems in Iraq, still they hope to live in Europe. So, this is the fault of UNHCR," Shourifi thundered.

Shourifi continued his tirade, while Mohammed Yahya, my translator for this interview and an exile himself, tried to keep up with Shourifi's venomous list of culprits. "And also, some of the Baathists who are here, they are against the Iraqi government and they tell the people not to go back. They made these rumors through the UN, and the UN encourages these rumors. So, too many Iraqis want to stay here!"

Mohammed Yahya translated the harsh words impassively. Shourifi hardly noticed Yahya, this Iraqi who had not accepted the return offer, while he spewed out his theories about why Iraqis were not signing up for the free government trips. "This will take the brains away from Iraq, and that is why I say that the UN is responsible for this!"

Glancing away from Shourifi's desk, I noticed the chaos of paperwork on every available surface. There were a few burn marks in the carpet from cigarettes stamped out by nervous men. An assistant shuffled into the office with more papers for Shourifi to sign, which he did without taking a break from his relentlessly upbeat assessment of Iraq. "We are a free country, a democratic country," he said, "We have 125 newspapers and 75 satellite channels. It's just the terrorists who are the problem." Shourifi did not mention that Iraq had reached a new milestone. By 2009, it was ranked as the most corrupt country in the Arab world, and the fourth most corrupt among all nations, by Transparency International, an international watchdog group. Baghdad had developed into a kleptocracy that rivaled Nigeria. Shourifi also neglected to say that Iraq was still a place of militias and unemployment, with intermittent bombings, kidnappings, and assassinations. Or that medical care remained far below pre-war standards. Or that electricity and water supplies were undependable at best. The capital was a cantonized city controlled by armed guards at checkpoints. The sectarian police force was deeply corrupt. There was no longer such a thing as a Baghdadi—just Sunnis or Shiites. An Iraqi could still be the wrong kind of Muslim for a particular neighborhood. Shourifi mentioned none of this.

If Shourifi had any compassion for the Iraqis living in desperate exile he did not show it. His attitude appeared to reflect that of his prime minister: Behind closed doors, Maliki routinely called the exiles "cowards" and "traitors" so often that many United Nations officials repeated the quote to me whenever I asked about the prime minister's seeming lack of compassion for the exile population. The theories for Maliki's poisonous observations divided into two camps. Maliki didn't understand the post-sectarian war trauma because his experiences were shaped by his protected seat in the Green Zone. Or his views were shaped by his own long experience in exile when the international community took little notice of Iraq's exiled politicians and he had to fend for himself. There was a third possibility. Many top officials knew the majority of exiles were Sunnis.

For Maliki, the mass exodus remained an inconvenient public relations problem. The half-hearted government program of promised cash inducements and free transport gave cover to charges that Maliki didn't want the exiles back. Neighboring countries and the international community had declared the Iraqi exodus a humanitarian crisis, but Maliki's message was of his country's recovery. The exiles, however, didn't believe a word of it. Their presence outside the country denied it.

Everyone knew that the Iraqi government had offered little support to Iraqi citizens who fled the country. A UNCHR telephone survey of Iraqis who had signed up for the government's return program showed that only 10 percent of the returnees got the promised cash. Apart from one transfer of $25 million for both Jordan and Syria, the Maliki government made no effort to ease the burden on regional neighbors that were hosting Iraqi citizens, or to alleviate the devastating living conditions with cash assistance for the exiles themselves.

This, too, was part of Iraq's failure at national reconciliation. A democratic nation should seek to protect all its citizens. Instead, the exiles concluded they had been abandoned by their government *because* the community was disproportionately Sunni and Christian.

"They don't trust the government yet," said Safa Rasul Hussein, the deputy national security advisor for the Iraqi government and a rare official willing to be critical of Baghdad policies. He believed that Iraq had to work harder to convince its citizens that they were welcome home and that the Maliki government had yet to get the return policy right. "Not many are coming back from the outside. It's the security and the whole situation. The complete package is not good enough. If we don't work on this, they won't come back at all." Safa Rasul had hoped that about 20 percent of the exile population would return by the end of 2008, a tipping point that would entice more exiles to return in even larger numbers. But the evidence was damning: By the end of 2008, barely 1 percent of the exile population had returned. In 2009, more Iraqis were leaving than coming back. Among the Iraqis still most keen to leave were those who had worked for the United States. At the U.S. embassy in Baghdad, a program to resettle them had a caseload so large that it took a year to schedule the first interview. More signed up every day.

Iraq was effectively a different country, transformed by the sectarian civil war. The Shiites had won, the Sunnis had lost. There was no getting around that. In the current political climate, there was little hope of restoring Baghdad's historic character, a city where Iraq's rich sectarian mix once lived side by side. Instead Baghdad had a distinctly Shiite spirit, on display during religious holidays when Shiite religious banners were hoisted over most of the city. Many of the Sunni mosques in the city were closed or in ruins.

"Iraq will be different for the Sunnis even if the security is good," said Safa Rasul frankly. He was one of a few high-ranking government officials who had not been part of the class of political exiles who now rule the country. Safa Rasul's political background, as an officer in Saddam's military with secret links to the Iraq's political dissidents, shaped his views on the future of Iraq and put him at odds with leading Shiite politicians. Moreover, he was from a prominent Shiite family and married to a Sunni. He acknowledged that the Maliki government wanted to ensure that Baghdad remained a predominantly Shiite capital. Iraqi government officials agreed that they wanted to reverse the brain drain, but there was no agreement on how to do that. The U.S. surge had reduced the violence in the capital, but there was an unintended political consequence. The Shiite-dominated power structure was free to pursue its own interests. Sunnis returning would find themselves part of a minority with no guarantees that their status would be protected.

For those considering a return to their old homes—according to World Bank figures, 60 percent of the exiles were home owners in Baghdad—more than a million cases of disputed ownership prevented any chance of a quick return, even assuming that the previous home was in a neighborhood considered safe. Iraqi exiles often protested that militia members had stolen their homes at gunpoint, or that squatters had moved in, or that their houses had been appropriated as part of a sectarian cleansing campaign. Others were forced to sell homes far below market value in illegal transactions at the height of the sectarian civil war. Tenants abandoned long-term lease agreements in the rush out of the country and landlords renegotiated the leases at higher prices to new residents, often from a rival sectarian group.

The International Office of Migration tried to quantify the scale of the problem with a housing survey among the internally displaced. The findings revealed that almost 70 percent of the IDPs said that their property was occupied by someone else without their permission or that they did not know the status of their property, suggesting that they considered it too dangerous to return to their old neighborhoods to find out. It was a staggering obstacle. Many who did return discovered that the homes their families had lived in for generations were simply no longer theirs.

The Iraqi government developed procedures to untangle the massive housing dilemma with two new orders: the Council of Ministers Decree 262 and the Prime Minister's Order 101. But the rules and procedures for reclaiming lost property applied only to those who had fled the country between January 2006 and January 2008. This window represented a period of unprecedented flight, but by setting dates, the government program left out certain constituencies. The threats against Christian minorities had continued after January 2008. And the larger population of exiles who had left the country between 2003 and 2006 were excluded entirely. By a UNHCR estimate there were 1.2 million Iraqis in this category, the majority Sunni.

The government's half-hearted property rights resolution was further evidence for those who believed that the old Iraq was irreparable. The clock could not be turned back. The country's new sectarian map, drawn by militias and terrorists, would endure. Arafat Jamal, the deputy representative of UNHCR in Amman, Jordan, described the Iraqi population in Jordan as highly professional people who would not consider going back without some resolution for their property claims and the reclamation of lost government jobs. "It's less dishonorable to be a refugee than to be out of work in Iraq," said Jamal. As for the Christian minorities in Amman, Jamal was convinced they would never return. By 2009, the European Union had stepped up resettlement quotas, promising places for as many as ten thousand Iraqis, mostly threatened Christians, despite appeals from Iraq that doing so would diminish the remaining Christian community and raise questions about its continued viability.

Three possible outcomes faced the refugees. Permanent integration in the host countries was one solution, but that had been rejected by the governments of Syria and Jordan where the overwhelming number of exiles resided. Another solution was resettlement in third countries—for example, America, Europe, and Australia. By 2009, the United States had resettled more than twenty thousand Iraqis and the EU and Canada had stepped up resettlement quotas, but even at this enhanced pace the backlog of cases would take more than a decade. The only practical solution for most Iraqi refugees was voluntary repatriation to Iraq, which remained dependent on the restoration of stability, the rule of law, and convincing political reconciliation. In the near term, it looked like a fantasy.

CONCLUSION: BAGHDAD

When I left Baghdad in September 2005, I was exhausted by the horrific violence of sectarian warfare. Like so many of the Iraqi exiles, I
too wanted out from a city that I knew as well as any other in the Arab
world. Four years later, six years after the American troops arrived on
Iraqi soil, I came back hoping to see differences. Perhaps the grim narrative of exile had begun to be reversed.

I noticed changes even before I landed. On the short flight from
Amman to Baghdad, the passengers still included many private contractors, a fraternity of Western men, mostly Americans and Brits,
with short hair and elaborate tattoos. But now the majority were Iraqi
families: children clutching backpacks, women in jeans, some with
loose head scarves, but others bare-headed, a sign that secular dress-
styles had made a comeback in the capital. The wartime landing, a
gut-wrenching corkscrew plane spin with the earth rushing up like a
crash before touchdown, had been replaced by a professionally smooth
glide on to the hot tarmac.

The baggage hall had the reassuring signals of normalcy: a large
wall poster advertising oil companies and American soft drinks. The
passengers waited quietly for the luggage carousel to spring to life. Remarkably, no one smoked, in keeping with a new health regulation to
keep the airport cigarette-free. The only obvious sign of the unsettled
nature of Iraq were the two hundred Ugandan contractors, dressed in

identical uniforms, sitting cross-legged on the floor in the departure hall waiting for exit papers before a flight to Kampala. Uganda's single private security agency, "Watertight Security Services," had been sending security guards to Iraq since 2007 with lucrative yearly contracts to provide 10,000 checkpoint guards.

The most dramatic change was in the airport departure routine. In 2005, the airport road was the most dangerous stretch of highway anywhere in the world. Four years later, the driver navigated our (nonetheless) armored car at normal speeds on roads busy with Iraqi drivers in late-model cars, secondhand pickup trucks piled with passengers, and battered white and orange taxi cabs. There was plenty of foot traffic on the streets, and shops and restaurants were open for business as we crossed the Tigris into Jadriyeh, the upscale neighborhood that was home to the small corps of Western journalists in the city.

The most visible legacy of the war was erected across the city in grey concrete. Ugly concrete ravines and mazes had saved lives but divided the population. The two-ton, eight-foot-tall barriers surrounded entire neighborhoods, disrupted traffic flows, cut off traditional markets from regular customers, and had become the cartography of the sectarian divide. In the first few days after my arrival, Prime Minister Nouri al-Maliki pledged to remove Baghdad's concrete labyrinth within forty days, a signal of his belief that his government had the violence under control and a message to the voters he needed if he was to remain prime minister after the national ballot in five months' time. Electricity, water, healthcare, and other government services had remained at levels that would sink a political campaign anywhere else. In Iraq, safety was so highly prized that Maliki's electoral future depended on the perception that he could deliver normality to a traumatized city. His image as the man who kept Baghdad safe had served him well in the recent provincial elections. Maliki's newly organized State of Law coalition had shed religious and sectarian language in the campaign and won votes for a more secular, more nationalist Iraq.

A heavy water tanker lumbered up al-Salhiya Street nineteen days after my return, part of the early summer morning traffic, inching along so slowly that the dozens of red plastic barrels tied to the truck bed barely quivered in the shimmering heat. The cars, with the giant tanker as the centerpiece of the procession, rolled along one of the main arteries of the city, four lanes of asphalt, past rows of high-rise apartments, past an Iraqi police checkpoint, one of more than two hundred across the city, past the remains of a stack of concrete security walls.

The final moments of the water tanker's journey were recorded on a security camera that had been installed by the Baghdad municipality high above the street across from the Foreign Ministry. It was a bright, sunny day and the sharp, clear images were recorded from this elevated position, after the water tanker's driver negotiated the checkpoint farther up the street. Did he chat with the police? Perhaps he joked with them, reminding one that he was a distant relative. These were the new ploys Iraqis used to speed up the security regime now that the Americans were no longer guarding Baghdad. Did the tanker driver offer a small bribe to smooth his way through a cursory search from police officers who had come to expect a share of graft collected in ever larger amounts by government officials with a service to sell? Or did these Iraqi guards anxiously check their watches, expecting the tanker driver to pass by this specific point in the city, the last potential obstacle in a mission that they supported? The security video provided no answers to questions repeatedly asked as its images were broadcast again and again on Iraqi state television over the coming days. Without those answers there was nothing to suggest the attacks would end.

The camera lens silently shattered as a thick brown cloud of dust, dirt, roadside debris, shards of glass, and body parts expanded into the air. The picture went black moments after the tanker driver blew himself into the memory of the city. More than one ton of explosives packed in the red water barrels loaded on his truck splintered the façade of the building, gouging a ten-foot crater in the parking lot. It was a little after 10:30 in the morning. This was the second massive suicide bomb of the day.

A few miles away, the concussions shook the office walls and rattled the windows; I felt the bang before I heard the blasts. From the top floor, with a broad view of Baghdad's low roofline, I could see the clouds of dark smoke billowing up from the massive explosions. It would be hours before anyone could piece together the details of what Iraqis would call Bloody Wednesday. This was mass murder on an ordinary workday, as the death count, the casualties, the horror inside the government ministries after glass and concrete imploded in meeting rooms and office cubicles, became clear. I thought of those very few Iraqi exiles who were considering coming home. What were they thinking now?

At least one hundred people died on Bloody Wednesday, and more than five hundred were wounded, in attacks aimed at the heart of the government. A feeling of disbelief enveloped Iraqis who had hoped the bad days were over. Across Baghdad, Maliki's security measures were denounced as folly, and increasingly Iraqis worried aloud that the Americans were leaving too soon. A columnist in the daily newspaper *al-Zaman* captured the city's mood by proclaiming: "These bombings exposed the nakedness of the government and the weakness of its security apparatuses which are not only incompetent but are steeped in corruption and bribery."

The prime minister quickly ordered the arrest of dozens of officers in Iraq's security service. Then he blamed a new alliance of Islamic extremists, ex-Baathists, and former regime loyalists. He lashed out at Syria, charging Damascus with complicity for what he said was providing a haven for the conspirators. His claims were impossible to access but his motives were clear. Every Iraqi faction blamed its enemies. Many Sunnis claimed Iran was behind the attack. It was an unmistakable warning, they said, to Prime Minister Maliki, who had recently broken with his former partners in a Shiite political alliance seen as most friendly to Tehran. More Iraqis blamed the political system itself. The biggest parties still had armed wings or militias at their disposal, and many Iraqis believed these groups were playing rough on the streets of Baghdad. Maliki's rivals would certainly benefit on Election Day if his claims to leadership by keeping Iraq safe were undermined. In October, when suicide bombers again struck at the Justice and Finance Ministries and the death toll exceeded that of the August bombings, Abbas Bayati, a Maliki supporter in Parliament, repeated demands for an international investigation: "We don't want these terrorist attacks to be ammunition for political disputes," he said. "The Sunnis accuse Iran and the Shiites accuse Syria. This is not good. We should deal with facts."

The facts that were most relevant were simply these: The bloody bombings failed to re-ignite sectarian revenge cycles because the bombers had made no distinction between the victims. Sunnis and Shiites were among the dead. The segregated neighborhoods mourned without reprisals.

But whatever nationalist sentiment in Baghdad existed was not yet strong enough to entice the exiles back. Iraq was a politically fragmented country, the prime minister still distrustful of those who had left. "He benefits from being perceived as a nationalist leader, but Maliki sees a Baathist behind every bush," explained Ryan Crocker, the American diplomat who had spent years interpreting Maliki's motives for the U.S. government. "He's worried that Baathism lurks in the hearts of many Sunni Arabs. It's constrained him. He believes that throughout Jordan and Syria, most are plotting his overthrow. It's not true. They are not his enemies."

"What we need [are] people in charge who really believe that those people should come home," Ayad al-Sammaraie, the Speaker of Parliament, told me. "If the government says we want the refugees to return but they do not protect them, they do not compensate them, they do not secure their life, their properties, their jobs, I mean, how would they come back?"

In this way the great shift of power in Iraq—in which the Sunnis had been largely removed from national, and subsequently regional, power—remains unresolved. Their eclipse is far from over, making a lasting Iraqi national reconciliation impossible. Sunnis still complain bitterly about the system known as *muhasasa*, ethno-sectarian quotas that ensure the majority of plum government jobs go to Shiites and Kurds. Even the Muslim prayers, televised daily on state-run television, come under *muhasasa* rules. Only the noon call-to-prayer is the Sunni version—a slight, but significant, difference. When calling the faithful, Muslims invoke God and the prophet Muhammed, but the Shiites add Ali, the Prophet's cousin, husband of his daughter Fatima, and a central figure in the Shiite faith. In the centuries-old divide in Islam, that one name, *Ali*, continues to be a major issue.

"There are a lot of mistakes and there are people who will go on about some little detail. They are not realistic." Ayad al-Sammaraie told me sharply, but then the Speaker looked uncomfortable as he reflected on what seemed like a minor controversy over televised prayers. These prayers, as well as the huge posters of Shiite Islam's holiest men that adorned the city, were less signs of religious fervor than of Shiite power in the city. A former engineer, Sammaraie had honed his English-language skills in Britain, where he had lived in exile for decades. He returned to Baghdad after the American invasion, joining a sectarian Sunni political movement. In Iraq's political equation, the Speaker's post goes to a Sunni Arab. Sammaraie had won the parliamentary ballot for the job partly because of his reputation as one of the prime minister's harshest critics. Maliki's enemies—Sunnis, Shiites, and Kurds—had rallied behind Sammaraie when the parliamentary speaker led a robust campaign to try to curb the prime minister's power.

"In the end, nobody can get everything he wants; others have rights, and others have demands as well." Sammaraie was expressing a logical reality but a credibility gap remained: How do you integrate people who don't yet trust each other?

"Well, I cannot say there is trust," Sammaraie persisted. "But let's say we are more realistic," he began when I asked him to explain Iraq's turn from a sectarian identity to a more national one. "We have to live together whether I trust the other party or I don't trust [them]. Ideally, I have to find a way to live [with them] and even find a way to improve the percentage of trust among us." It sounded reasonable.

But one victim of the Sunni eclipse was likely to be Maliki himself. Ahead of the national elections, Shiite politicians, including Maliki, were courting Sunni partners, a kind of political speed dating, to find willing and acceptable partners to provide nationalist credentials. The election law, ratified by the Parliament, reflected the more secular mood by banning the use of religious images in the campaign. The exiles would be allowed to vote in Iraqi embassies abroad. Maliki needed the secular, middle-class Iraqis to back him at the polls. But he failed to co-opt prominent Sunnis to join his ticket. He needed exactly the kinds of people who had begun leaving Iraq in 2005 and were now scattered across the Middle East and around the world. They were unlikely to rally to his cause.

Among the exiles whom I knew well, many had already voted with their passports. Mohammed Yahya, the veterinarian-turned-translator, had written to me every few weeks from Damascus to say there was still nothing new in his case. Then, one day in the winter of 2009, he announced he had his plane tickets and he and his family would be resettled in Maryland. He believed that his neighborhood in the Iraqi capital was still a dangerous place for him and his family because of his work with a Western news agency and his former employment with the American government. The power of the Mahdi army had diminished in his neighborhood of Hurriyah, but the sectarian cleansing that took place in 2007 had barely been reversed. When I finally saw him and his family in the new apartment in the Maryland suburbs, he smiled more than I remembered.

The most cheerful messages came regularly from Nezar Hussein, who had returned to Baghdad to try to resume filmmaking there, keeping the promise he made to himself. He saw an opportunity to document the search for a new identity in his homeland. He was determined to make the best of Baghdad. "The life rhythm here is really crazy," he e-mailed. "The people here are thirsty for life and they will do anything just to feel alive once again. I feel reborn." He finally won a contract from a company in Dubai to make a series of documentaries. Art was his passport and if life became unbearable for him in Iraq, I hoped he could find a way out to save himself again.

By 2009, Iraqi refugees were the largest group resettled in the United States. But the lobbying coalition of NGOs and refugee agencies that had campaigned to increase the resettlement quotas now had a newly pressing concern. The U.S. program, strained by the global economic downturn, was failing the new arrivals. The system depended on the availability of easy employment for newcomers: They were expected to find work and become self-sufficient within months. But the financial crash had brought the system close to collapse, with Iraqis falling into poverty and homelessness. The International Rescue Committee, the largest resettlement agency in the country, raised the alarm in a report: "Iraqi Refugees in America: In Dire Straights." America was hardly a safe and secure haven, according to the IRC. "A large number of resettled refugees are widows, most with young children, who arrive grieving and alone. These widows, including many who have no employment experience, are expected to find a job and support themselves and their families shortly after arrival."

There was no way to predict how the Iraqis would adapt in the United States. In some cases, success was based on random placement. Texas and Arizona were particularly tough states for resettlement because the job market was the tightest in the failing economy. Waleed Arshad, a graduate of Baghdad's Institute of Fine Arts, had worked on an American army base for two years painting warning signs in Arabic—"HALT, DO NOT COME CLOSER THAN 100 METERS. DEADLY FORCE WILL BE USED"—until he convinced the soldiers to let him paint their portraits. He painted thousands of oil portraits and was even allowed to have a small gallery on the base. When the death threats started, he moved his family to Damascus, registered for resettlement, and made a living selling paintings to diplomats. I had seen him often in the Syrian capital, while he and his family waited for the approvals he believed would change his life for the better.

In Texas, the American economy was now Arshad's greatest enemy. The Texas relief agency in charge of his resettlement had cut off his benefits after two months and, in danger of homelessness, he had reached out to American friends who had raised money to help him out for a few months. His new paintings, of loss and despair, reflected the status of the wider community, but went largely unsold. He got part-time work cleaning houses in Dallas but it was never enough to cover the rent and food for his two children. The brain drain in Iraq had wasted Iraqi talent in one country and now would waste human capital in another. Arshad talked about going back to Damascus, even considered a return to Baghdad, but his friends counseled him to stick it out in Texas.

Iraqis with acute medical problems, from diabetes to war injuries, were often settled in Massachusetts, where they qualified for healthcare as soon as they arrived. But others landed in the United States with documents that gave no indication of medical complications. Some went straight from the airport of their new home city to the emergency room at the local hospital. Aid workers were often unaware that the new arrivals, suffering from dangerously high blood pressure or debil-itating chest pains, were showing the symptoms of the ills of war.

Another factor that changed the odds for Iraqis resettling in the United States was the presence of a sponsor, a family member, or a friend who agreed to support the new arrivals. Ali Jabber, an Iraqi translator for a U.S. military police company in Iraq, contacted me through Facebook to say that he'd made it to Antioch, California. Ali and his wife had lived in a shabby hotel room in Amman, Jordan. In self-imposed confinement—cooped up in this tiny space for almost two years—they were afraid to venture outside for fear of deportation by the Jordanian police. Ali's American sponsor, Juan Estrada, a ser-geant with the 870 military police company in the California National Guard, had taken on an extraordinary commitment.

When I first met the couple in Jordan, Ali told me that Estrada was his "American father." He showed me a copybook with sums carefully written down. Estrada wired money each month to pay the hotel bills during the long wait for resettlement. The dollar figures represented something much bigger. Ali was proud that the American soldier was his patron, his only lifeline in Jordan. When Ali and his wife were fi-nally resettled in California, Estrada offered them a room in his home. They lived with him for three months. When I think of Iraqi refugees arriving in the United States, and of the vast American ignorance of their plight, Ali's story seems to offer hope of redemption on both sides. But it is not quite so simple.

A year after Ali had been resettled I called Estrada in California. "Nothing was hard for [Ali]. We were together most of the time. I was holding his hand through the resettlement. I got him a cellphone.

I drove him around. So, yeah, I was his 'Dad.' I was carrying him the whole time," Estrada confirmed. The two men had formed a strong bond in Iraq, the young Iraqi Shiite, with a recent B.A. in English from the University of Baghdad, and the experienced sergeant from California on his first deployment to the Middle East.

"I knew how he was going to feel—totally lost," said Estrada. He had been overcome with the same sense of being "totally lost" in Iraq until Ali had explained Iraqi culture and translated Arabic. He had risked his life for Juan Estrada and the military police company from California. "He has learned Americanisms and I've learned about Arabs and Islam," Estrada told me, as he described a friendship that had changed and grown. "He's made me smarter, more intelligent and made me realize our ignorance. It was a tragic mistake. That's my opinion, anyway," he said, about the invasion of Iraq. Both men had paid a price.

Two years after my first interview with Ali Jabber and his wife, Sura, I drove east out of San Francisco on a rainy afternoon for the two-hour trip to the delta region, to attend the annual reunion picnic of the 870 military police unit and their families. Ali's success in navigating American culture had brought him a driver's license, a car, and a steady job. He knew these men well enough to accept their gentle teasing over his awkward confusion in those early days, mistaking a traffic jam for a checkpoint, his wonderment at the overwhelming choices of cheese in a California supermarket. They accepted his observations about some of the oddities of American culture and pledged to finance his further education over the campfire.

Ali and Sura were part of this National Guard family now. The former Iraqi translator joined in the volleyball games and learned the traditions of American barbeques. Sura also played hard along with the men. Her transformation was remarkable: from the shy young woman in a head scarf I had met in Jordan to a confident English speaker, smashing the ball over the net, hair flying, uncovered.

Ali's family was still in Iraq, and he followed the news as best he could on the Internet during the breaks from his job as a caretaker at a yacht club. Estrada, still on active duty, volunteered for redeployment to Iraq. He felt an obligation, he said, to be a part of the withdrawal operation. "Most of them are against it," he told me, referring to his friends in the Guard. "Our bond is close. They don't believe in the mission. I'm not getting a pat on the back." His answer hung in the California dusk. These men were as close to him as anyone on earth. They had gone to war together and been transformed by the experience. Most had overcome the war trauma; at least one had not. Many had left the military as soon as they could so they wouldn't have to go back to Iraq. Estrada felt keenly that he was needed there to finish the job they had all started. The rest of the country might not care, but Estrada did.

"The Iraq war is a chapter in my life. Iraq is part of my life. Does that make sense? And that's because of them," he said of the Iraqi couple whom he saw as a personal responsibility. His sense of duty had strained his own family to the breaking point.

"They came to live with us. I set them up in a room in the house, this little room in this peaceful world. Near my family, but my family didn't accept that. I really did make a choice at that point," Estrada said, recounting the painful split with his wife and college-aged son and daughter. They never did understand why he brought the Iraqis home. The long separations of military life had been a strain. The new guests led to the final break. Estrada bought a new house for himself and his new Iraqi family. His American wife and children were convinced this was some kind of delayed reaction to the war.

"I said hey, this is the right thing to do. I'm sorry you are uncomfortable and you don't understand Arabs or whatever that might be, you know. There were some sides to my family I hadn't seen before— ignorance and a lack of tolerance. Even in our reunion, Ali is the reminder, a good reminder, of something good we did over there."

What life had become for Estrada was clear when I went to his suburban home the next day. Ali and Sura were there, too, comfortable, in front of a wide-screen TV. They came to stay on the weekends in a re-creation of the close family ties from home. When Estrada deployed to Iraq, Ali and Sura would move in full-time. I could imagine them worrying over Estrada and keeping up with frequent phone calls and e-mails in ways that Estrada's American family could not or would not do.

"Ali brought it all to a head. I feel bad from the father-husband perspective, but for the citizen-soldier part, I did the right thing. My family. They didn't get the war, what we owe those people. It's hard to explain that. They just don't know," said Estrada. He was quiet for a moment, and in the silence I thought about the Iraqi exiles I had met over the past few years. Estrada had faced up to the essential question that I had been seeking to answer: What do we owe "those people"? His answer, delivered with courage and conviction, was simple: We owe them a home, because we took theirs away. "It's been an epiphany," he finally said.

I asked Juan if Ali and his wife seemed like permanent parts of his life now.

"Yeah. I've been dancing around that for a while. But, yeah. They are in my life forever. It's not a problem. That's how it is."

AUTHOR'S NOTE:
CHANGED IDENTITIES

The names of some of the Iraqis portrayed in this book have been changed, and the details of their lives altered to shield their identities. This does not make their stories any less true, but protects them from retribution, which, in many cases, was the cause of their flight from Baghdad.

ACKNOWLEDGMENTS

When I arrived in Baghdad in May 2003, I had no idea that Iraq would become the longest assignment of my career. I owe an enormous debt to those who helped me see the country and the rest of the region not as I wished, but as it is. When I've gotten it right, it is because of them; the mistakes, errors of judgment, or other faults in this work are my sole responsibility. So many people shared their time and insights that I list them alphabetically, because there is no way to rank their contributions. Samir Aita, Rime Alaf, Waleed Arshad, Oliver August, Ali Badr, Bob Baer, George Baghdadi, Henri Barkey, Mohammed Bazzi, Annia Ciezadlo, Hydar Daffar, Borzou Daragahi, Adeed Dawisha, Ruthie Epstein, Andrew Exum, Ali Fadil, Isra Abdul Hadi, Ibrahim Hamidi, Peter Harling, Joost Hilterman, Azza Humadi, Feisal al-Istrabadi, Ahlan al-Jabouri, Kirk Johnson, Brian Katulis, Michael Kocher, Leith Kubba, Josh Landis, Suha Maayeh, Mona Mahmood, Nezar Mhawi, Abdullah Mizead, Roula Nasrallah, Jorgen Nielsen, Sam Parker, Vanessa Parra, Volker Perthes, Damien Quinn, Khaled Saffuri, Leena Saidi, Omar Salih, Ahmed Salkini, Nadeem Shehadi, Liz Sly, Wendell Steavenson, Andrew Tabler, Samir al-Taqi, Amelia Templeton, Nabil al-Tikriti, Melissa Winkler, Fareed Yaseen, Kristel Younis, and Mohammed Yuaid.

I owe an additional debt of gratitude to my "readers," whose reactions and comments along the way helped me make the text richer:

Rick Davis, Carol Sakoian, Anna Husarska, John Felton, Peter Pringle, Karen Deyoung, Madeleine Segall-Marx, Julia Redpath Bailey, and Ally Gordon.

I would also like to thank friends and colleagues who supported my work, did not mention my long absences, and mostly listened to my stories: Fred Kaplan and Brooke Gladstone, Eleanor Randolph, Robin Lustig and Ruth Kelsey, Laurie Garrett, Bill Moyers, Joanne Levine, Madhulika Sikka, and my family, Jeannie Amos, Dorothy Amos, John Amos, and my father, John, who listened for as long as he could remember.

Thanks to Robert Rosenthal and Christa Schafenberg at the Center for Investigative Reporting.

Thanks to Loren Jenkins for inadvertently launching me on this journey when he sent me to Baghdad in 2003 as a fill-in and then supported the continued coverage of Iraqi exiles, and to Doug Roberts, my editor at National Public Radio, who made sure the scripts were polished and the Arabic correct.

Thanks to Larry Weissman, who knew I could do this book before I did, and to the people at PublicAffairs: Susan Weinberg, Peter Osnos, Tessa Shanks, Melissa Raymond, and especially Clive Priddle, who is an extraordinarily generous editor, a man of wit and wisdom who made me laugh as well as think.

INDEX

Shannon Taggart

Deborah Amos's reports can be heard on NPR's award-winning *Morning Edition, All Things Considered,* and *Weekend Edition.* For a decade she reported for television news, including ABC's *Nightline* and *World News Tonight* and the PBS programs *NOW with Bill Moyers* and *Frontline.* Amos has won many awards, including the Edward Weintal Prize for Diplomatic Reporting in 2009. She spent 1991–1992 as a Nieman Fellow at Harvard University, and is a member of the Council on Foreign Relations. She lives in New York City.

PublicAffairs is a publishing house founded in 1997. It is a tribute to the standards, values, and flair of three persons who have served as mentors to countless reporters, writers, editors, and book people of all kinds, including me.

I. F. STONE, proprietor of *I. F. Stone's Weekly*, combined a commitment to the First Amendment with entrepreneurial zeal and reporting skill and became one of the great independent journalists in American history. At the age of eighty, Izzy published *The Trial of Socrates*, which was a national bestseller. He wrote the book after he taught himself ancient Greek.

BENJAMIN C. BRADLEE was for nearly thirty years the charismatic editorial leader of *The Washington Post*. It was Ben who gave the *Post* the range and courage to pursue such historic issues as Watergate. He supported his reporters with a tenacity that made them fearless and it is no accident that so many became authors of influential, best-selling books.

ROBERT L. BERNSTEIN, the chief executive of Random House for more than a quarter century, guided one of the nation's premier publishing houses. Bob was personally responsible for many books of political dissent and argument that challenged tyranny around the globe. He is also the founder and longtime chair of Human Rights Watch, one of the most respected human rights organizations in the world.

·   ·   ·

For fifty years, the banner of Public Affairs Press was carried by its owner Morris B. Schnapper, who published Gandhi, Nasser, Toynbee, Truman, and about 1,500 other authors. In 1983, Schnapper was described by *The Washington Post* as "a redoubtable gadfly." His legacy will endure in the books to come.

Peter Osnos, *Founder and Editor-at-Large*